IMPALA

1958 — 2000

text by **DAN BURGER**
photography by **ROBERT GENAT**

MBI Publishing Company

First published in 2000 by MBI Publishing Company, 729 Prospect Avenue, PO Box 1, Osceola, WI 54020-0001 USA

MBI Publishing Company books are also available at discounts in bulk quantity for industrial or sales-promotional use. For details write to Special Sales Manager at Motorbooks International Wholesalers & Distributors, 729 Prospect Avenue, PO Box 1, Osceola, WI 54020-0001 USA.

Library of Congress Cataloging-in-Publication Data

Burger, Dan.
   Impala, 1958-2000 / Dan Burger & Robert Genat.
     p. cm.—(American classics)
   Includes index.
   ISBN 0-7603-0805-5 (pbk. : alk. paper)
      1. Impala automobile—History. I. Genat, Robert,
   II. Title. III. American classics (Osceola, Wis.)

TL 215.I43 B87 2000
629.222'2—dc21   00-057886

On the front cover: Fresh for 1958 was the Impala, Chevrolet's top-of-the-line full-size car. Impala was available as a coupe or a convertible and offered buyers a combination of sportiness, luxury, and prestige. *Zone Five Photo*

On the frontispiece: Impala's legendary SS emblem, the symbol of high performance. *Zone Five Photo*

On the title page: To many, the 1963 Impala is the most handsome Chevrolet model manufactured in the 1960s. Its clean, light design makes it a favorite among collectors. *Zone Five Photo*

On the back cover: Although Chevrolet's new Caprice displaced the Impala as the top dog for 1966, Impala was no slouch. With a distinctive body and big V-8 power, Impala continued to attract attention and buyers. *Zone Five Photo*

Edited by Keith Mathiowetz
Designed by Jim Snyder

Printed in China

CONTENTS

ACKNOWLEDGMENTS

No author has ever written a book alone. One's name may be printed on the cover, but many people have an influence on what gets printed on the pages. History is only concrete when it comes to dates and places and quantifiable numbers. Much remains subject to interpretation. As an author, I attempt to sort through it all to provide the information that sums it up with the greatest accuracy and with insights that haven't been laid down in print before. Like any other compilation of facts and stories, this is my interpretation of what they mean and my selection of what is most significant.

I talked with members of the General Motors design group who were involved with Chevrolet styling from the 1950s through the 1990s. Their insights and recollections add a great deal of flavor to this Impala story. From those whom I spoke with, one person in particular was especially friendly, accessible, and always helpful—Chuck Jordan. Chuck's career at General Motors spanned the Impala era, and it overlapped the careers of Harley Earl and Bill Mitchell—the two most influential designers in the history of GM. Chuck arrived at General Motors in 1949 fresh out of the Massachusetts Institute of Technology and eventually became the vice president of design. He retired from GM in 1992. Chuck shared many hours with me talking automotive design and history. For this I am most grateful. His perspectives played a big role in how this book turned out; however, it would be wrong to equate this book with Chuck Jordan's view of the highs and lows of Impala history. It is not my intent to make this book appear as though it is a reflection of Chuck Jordan's point of view.

I also thank General Motors designers and executives Dave Holls, Ed Taylor, George Moon, Blaine Jenkins, Ed Donaldson, Don Laskey, and Warren Reinecker. Each provided valuable insights that factored into the content of this book.

Outside of this group of talented designers, who had the jobs that most car enthusiasts dream of having, there were Impala experts like Robert Snowden and Danny Howell from the Late Great Chevy Club. In the past 20 years they have seen more Impalas than probably anyone else on the planet.

Thanks also to Julia Daniel at the Chevrolet Archives; Dan Hubbert, Carolyn Landrum, and Nancy Libby at Chevrolet Public Relations; John Mahoney, a Chevy engine technical expert; Bill Hyde, an air suspension engineer; and Chevy enthusiasts Bob Hurst, Bob Ford, and Jerry Mull.

Owners of the beautiful Impalas that were photographed for this book include: Bob Carter, Tony and Joyce Duarte, Stuart Clark, Marvin and Sheryl Johnson, Bob Billings, Louise Bent, Mike Harvey, Kathy Miller, Vergel Sandifer, Mike Komo, Jerry and Billie Bowland, Tom Geiman, Jerome Ruzicka, Steve Halluska, and Sonny and Carol Hale.

I especially thank Robert Genat. His exceptional photography makes this a pleasure to look at, even if you don't read the words. And his diligence in ferreting out photos through sources such as the General Motors Archives and the Late Great Chevy Club has added an historic perspective that provides greater depth and insight into the Impala story.

—*Dan Burger*

The Fruits of Passion

"There are no shortcuts to any place worth going."

—Anonymous

The Impala was an automobile born into an age of great excitement and imagination. The space age was upon us, and the heretofore impossible was not only possible, it was real.

Automobiles were central to it all. The era was loaded with prosperity, high expectations, and an increased desire to go new places and see new things. Our cars were our rocket ships for the exploration of new personal frontiers. They seemed to drive on a pathway to the stars.

The imagery was great. Fly to the moon or pack up the family and drive to Florida. Cars expanded our earthbound universe while rockets propelled us into the space age. Adventure awaited, and more and more people were setting out to find it.

The automobile was transitioning from machine to convenience. And cars were given great names. A model number or the designations Custom and DeLuxe were too generic for these times. Names had to evoke passion and imagination—Galaxie and Meteor, Bonneville and Fury. These were exciting times, and the cars reflected them; these were cars that could shoot a stream of sparks across the night sky.

Of all the great machines that set fire to the super hot automotive scene that spurted from the fantastic 1950s, none could go the distance with the Chevrolet Impala. During its prime, it was center of the automotive solar system. And Impala still reigns as the best-selling full-size American nameplate of all time.

The Impala took people by surprise. When introduced in 1958, it was presented as a special edition Bel Air. Everyone knew the Bel Air was the finest Chevrolet you could buy. So what was the Impala? Something better yet? Yes. The Impala caused a commotion whenever it rolled into view. At rest it had a certain degree of elegance. Not coincidentally, it had a bit of Cadillac in its bloodlines. And with the performance-oriented engine options, it could run with and past cars that previously looked down on the lowly Chevrolet. Remember, all Chevys were powered by six cylinders just four years earlier.

People started taking the Impalas home in the fall of 1957, and the loyal following grew to record numbers within a blink of automotive history. In a matter of just a few years, the Impala sprinted past its contemporaries and the

most popular cars in history until that time, to become America's car.

In 1956 the interstate highway system set in motion the construction of great superhighways. Backed by the federal government, these modern highways ushered in a new era of auto travel that promised high-speed travel on 42,500 miles of limited-access concrete roadways. The bane of motorists, single-lane roads and stop-and-go traffic-light snarls, were planned right into extinction.

Of course, the 12-year plan took twice that long to actually complete, and by the time it was finished most metropolitan areas had suburban sprawl that flooded even the superhighways. Single lane–, signal light–induced traffic jams evolved into multi-lane gridlock. The road to Helena (or somewhere like that) is paved with good intentions. And, without a doubt, the allure of high speed and nonstop travel has always been a great seduction.

Not only did the interstates make long-distance travel faster, and therefore more appealing, but the modern, wide, multi-laned roads were the perfect accompaniment for cars that were bigger and more powerful. A car that could run all day at 60 or even 70 miles per hour meant bragging rights for the head of the household that was seeing all that America had to offer. Just getting there was good, but "did you make good time" played a big part in pride of ownership.

The interstate highway project of the 1950s was one of the great engineering accomplishments of that era. More people had more leisure time and more money to spend. The automobile was the most common benefactor. To the previous generation, owning a car carried status. By the late 1950s, owning a fancier model, a symbol of success, and traveling to far-off destinations in comfort was the new status.

The auto industry was in a frenzy. In the decade of the 1950s, motor vehicle registrations soared from 49 million to 71 million, and the total number of miles driven shot up from 450 million miles to 700 million miles. Without question this was a nation that enjoyed letting the good times roll, especially on the highways.

It was also an era of increasing emphasis on fashion as the middle class grew faster than it had at any other time in history. The automakers, particularly General

Motors, were fashion-minded as well. Yearly model changes played a big role in sales as people clamored for the latest thing in styling, and didn't want to be caught "behind the times." Anyone who considers the 1950s a bland decade need only look at the imagination and creativity that was unleashed in the auto industry during this decade. Manufacturers that were financially unable or philosophically unwilling to play this game, largely the smaller independent companies, suffered as a result. "Bigger is better" not only applied to the cars that were being built, but to the dominance of the corporations doing the building.

The Chevrolet Division of General Motors believed in the bigger-is-better theory. The Impala proved its viability. As a low-cost, high-volume automobile with tremendously loyal customers, Chevrolet had a huge market that was eager to buy bigger, faster, and more luxurious cars. The Impala was the result of giving the people what they wanted, and Chevy kicked butt with it. The Impala dominated. It rolled up huge numbers throughout the 1960s.

But Chevy wasn't completely blinded by that philosophy. Until the introduction of the Corvair in 1960, the only Chevrolets were full-size Chevrolets. Two years after this rear-engined, rear-wheel-drive compact Corvair, Chevrolet introduced a more conventional compact, the Chevy II. By 1964, Chevrolet was eager to develop another inroad into the smaller, lighter auto market with the Chevelle. Diversification continued with the Camaro and the Monte Carlo.

Throughout that decade of transformation, Impala led the Chevrolet Division despite all the additional products being brought forth. It built and then maintained both a performance image and a luxury image, even though challengers from within Chevrolet, General Motors, and the other car manufacturers became more numerous. Its appeal was far beyond that of any other nameplate—so much so that brand loyalty actually migrated from Chevrolet to Impala.

Even by the tail end of the 1960s and the beginning of the 1970s, when the Impala grew too big and heavy to maintain its performance edge, its popularity remained strong. Despite being knocked down a rung on the luxury ladder by Caprice, Impalas regularly outsold their upscale sibling. That never happened after Impala replaced Bel Air. Impala ruled.

It wasn't until the mid-1970s—after the Oil Embargo, the gas price hikes, and the emission-control regulations—that the full-size Chevy found itself too big for its surroundings. Youthful buyers, who once eagerly embraced Impala, turned away. There was a general mistrust of big business and big government, and consumers refused to buy big cars. Bigger was definitely not better. General Motors was a perfect target for anti-establishment

thinking. Impala was a perfect symbol for all that. It didn't mesh well with the "Age of Aquarius" mindset. Therefore, Impala's segment of the automotive world became somewhat of a dead-end street. Times had changed. Not only was bigger no longer better, bigger was the enemy.

Of course, you may have noticed that not everyone in America thinks the same way. The economic, governmental, and social circumstances may have cost Impala youthful buyers, but there were still plenty of people who believed that what was good for General Motors was good for the USA. For them, Chevy was as American as baseball, hot dogs, and apple pie. (I'll bet you already heard that from somewhere, right?)

Inevitably the road led to downsizing, and although the Impala survived, and continued to put up big numbers for several years, it was never the same. By this time it had lost its luster, and if Chevy had something new, something different, something exciting to offer, it wasn't going to be introduced as an Impala.

Those who grew up with the Impala, and the excitement that was generated by the automotive world whenever new models were unveiled, had become dulled by what the auto industry had become. The shine had definitely come off the diamond. Imagination and creativity that had once been poured into designs that inspired were channeled in other directions. It resulted in safer, more fuel-efficient, more environmentally sensitive automobiles. But unfortunately it also resulted in cars completely devoid of passion and excitement. It was as if one day, back around 1972 or so, the music died and the spotlights were turned off.

At least that's how the automotive enthusiasts feel. And for the Impala enthusiast, it was disappointing that the spotlight was no longer shining on Impala. It had become the aging star. Its brightest years were behind it. Image may not be everything, but in the automotive marketplace no one goes far without it.

After Chevrolet dropped the Impala nameplate in 1984, there was little mourning for the passing of the biggest, most widely recognized name in the history of automotive model identification. Too many years with too little attention reduced Chevrolet's greatest brand name, its greatest triumph, to the equivalent of yesterday's news. The country was in the midst of the worst economic recession to never be called a depression. Car sales were few and far between, especially compared to early 1970s and mid-1960s bonanzas, so the Impala was not really missed. The value of its name and its image was somehow not recognized.

It was surprising then that 10 years later someone at Chevrolet had an epiphany. Performance sells cars. Image sells cars. All it took was a look back at Chevrolet's most dominant car in its most dominant era. What did they find? The Impala SS. So like a bolt out of the blue, the

Impala SS was back. And so was automotive enthusiasm for a lot of the folks who experienced it the first time around—that being almost 30 years earlier.

The 1994–1996 Impala SS was a huge success, but not because it sold 150,000 cars a year like the original one did in the mid-1960s. This incarnation was a very limited production model with what has become a cult-like following. But the real reason it was a success is because it proved Chevrolet still had a soul and a passion for building cars. To build and maintain an image, Chevrolet can't rely solely on the Corvette. The Camaro isn't enough. It can prosper greatly by using the Impala name wisely. There's still magic in that name, and if Chevy wants people to become passionate about its most recent Impala (model year 2000), it should spend some time looking back at all the right things the company did in the era when Impala was king.

When Impala Was King

Year	Totals
1960	587,345
1961	555,942
1962	778,607
1963	894,868
1964	873,327
1965	1,068,614
1966	801,093
1967	721,271
1968	771,371
1969	772,302
TOTAL	7,824,740

Weighing the Options

"Nothing great in the world has ever been accomplished without passion."

—G. W. F. Hegel

Chevrolet scored big with a series of sensational achievements in the 1950s. It was a decade of dominance. The Chevy bow-tie emblem seemed to be everywhere—television, magazines, billboards, and subsequently on the minds of millions of Americans. When it came to hits, not even a combination of Elvis and the New York Yankees could top Chevrolet.

Beginning in 1950, the Bel Air became Chevy's big stick. It stirred the public by introducing the two-door hardtop to the low-priced field. The Bel Air was a breakthrough car for Chevy—it smashed the style barrier, drawing Chevrolet closer to more luxurious makes and models. That narrowing of the gap between the low-priced and the luxurious became an increasingly critical element in Chevrolet popularity as the decade progressed.

Another log on this fire was the debut of the Powerglide automatic transmission in 1950. It also boosted Chevy prestige by adding yet another engineering advancement that was once proprietary to the fine-car

The reverse-slant C-pillar (where the roof meets the rear quarter panel) was an idea seen on several of the General Motors Motorama show cars, including the 1956 Impala Motorama car. It was also used on GM's higher-priced cars of this vintage.
Zone Five Photo

11

Although there is no evidence that Chevrolet was interested in producing a Corvette that could accommodate more than two passengers, the Motorama Impala, with its Corvette influence, looks a lot better than the first four-passenger Thunderbird. *1978–1999 GM Corp. Used with permission of GM Media Archives*

The public introduction of the Chevrolet Impala took place in 1956 when the one-of-a-kind Impala show car debuted at the General Motors Motorama. The sporty four-passenger coupe had a strong Corvette flavor, and was referred to as the Corvette Impala in some of the motoring press. *1978–1999 GM Corp. Used with permission of GM Media Archives*

field. By the mid-1950s, Chevy was offering power brakes, power windows, and power seats. With Bel Air reigning supreme in the Chevrolet lineup, its reputation grew firecracker hot. Then the long-awaited V-8 burst onto the scene, and once again, Bel Air basked in the glow of a monumental achievement. When Chevy was referred to as "The Hot One," it was the Bel Air that most often took the spotlight and acknowledged the applause.

Chevrolet was on a roll, and it wanted the whole world to know it. Yes, the Bel Air was jalapeno hot, but Chevy was ready once again to turn up the heat. The dominantly influential Harley Earl was the GM commander-in-chief of design. His preferred style is best seen in the Chevys, Pontiacs, Buicks, Oldsmobiles, and Cadillacs of the early 1950s. The bigger, more expensive models continued to demonstrate his penchant for bigger, heavier, more luxurious automobiles. But the lower-priced cars in the GM armada, especially Chevrolet, continued to pursue the high-price cars in terms of size and horsepower and convenience items. Performance, comfort, and all the outward

When Impala joined the 1958 Chevrolet lineup, it was the top of the line, but officially considered a Bel Air series car. That first year it was only available as a hardtop coupe and a convertible. *1978–1999 GM Corp. Used with permission of GM Media Archives*

The Impala interiors were much more colorful and elaborate than those of other Chevy models. Chrome end panels on the front seats were one of the extra details that added distinction to this upscale Chevrolet. *Late Great Chevy Collection*

trimmings that signaled prestige were being brought to Chevrolet models, with the intent of keeping Chevrolet buyers who otherwise might be tempted to move up to Pontiac or Buick. The strategy provided a bounty for Chevrolet, but it was beginning to blur the distinction among GM brands.

When the stylized script with crossed flags and a leaping Impala was first affixed to the rear flanks of a 1958 full-size Chevrolet, the message was clear: Chevrolet was going all out to build an upscale, Cadillac-like automobile at a price within the means of the average working-class family. It was the American dream on four wheels—success and status in the family garage.

The Impala was originally conceived as a Bel Air executive coupe. Plymouth had capitalized on this idea with the introduction of the performance-oriented Fury in mid-1956. And Ford made a similar move when it evolved the Thunderbird into a four-seater in 1958 and introduced the Galaxie in 1959. Both Plymouth and Ford had redesigned models for 1957, cars that were substantially bigger and more powerful. Chevrolet's command of that arena came in 1958. Styling was dramatically different—much more Cadillac influenced than ever before. The timing and the execution were nearly perfect. It launched the Impala on a

run that would dominate for decades and was truly the birth of a giant.

Before the Impala took over the reins of Chevrolet leadership, it previewed as a Motorama show car in 1956. General Motors devised the Motoramas as a traveling showcase for their cars. The Motoramas not only increased sales and brand awareness, but they were clearly an exclamation point in demonstrating GM's superiority. The shows were huge spectacles—traveling extravaganzas of fantastic displays, lavish decorations, stage shows, audio-video, and live entertainment. They were held in multiple locations across the country, and they provided blockbuster publicity for the entire GM production model lineup. In 1956 there were Motoramas in New York, Miami, Los Angeles, San Francisco, and Boston. The attendance at these shows topped 2.3 million. The mid-1950s sales records created boundless enthusiasm and sparked the concepts for cars that followed in two or three years.

Always in the spotlight at these shows were the fantastic dream cars created by Earl and the inspired imaginations of the colossal GM design team, which numbered around 1,100 at that time. Creativity was unleashed and nothing seemed out of the realm of possibility. Each division had

After eight successful years as the top Chevrolet, the Bel Air stepped aside as Impala took on the most prestigious role, which included top billing in most of the advertising. Bragging rights were not overlooked as a reason to step up to Impala.

Chevrolet designers wanted the car to have a hint of Cadillac. In some years this was more evident than in others. The front-end design on the 1958 Chevrolet could have worked just as easily on a Cadillac. *Zone Five Photo*

cars of the future that foretold great things to come. Earl told his designers, "Do all you can. Don't hold anything back. If you do, it will be obsolete tomorrow." GM estimated that the cost of each hand-built dream car was between $200,000 and $250,000.

The Impala show car could accurately be described as a five-passenger sports car, or maybe better described in the European lexicon as a grand touring car. It was built on a 116.5-inch wheelbase and measured 202 inches overall. Although it was stylishly low and sleek, it was designed to carry three passengers in front and two in the rear. The design borrowed liberally from the Corvette identity, with the grille and integral bumper being the most obvious resemblance. Up front, the forward portion of the hood and headlight/front fender treatments were also strongly flavored by Corvette. The rear fender design and wrap-around-style bumper were also similar to the 1956 production Corvette's. Chrome wire wheels with knock-off hubs added to the sports car appeal.

Like the production Corvette, the two-toned blue Impala show car was made of fiberglass. The roof and glass area appeared much like the production model 1958 Impala, except the windshield extended upward and into the roof as a way of presenting a more panoramic view, a concept that was borrowed from the 1955 Biscayne

Motorama dream car. The reverse-slant C-pillar was later seen on the 1957 Cadillac, Oldsmobile, and Buick, and the 1958 Chevrolet and Pontiac. The spear-shaped side trim of the show car also was carried over to the production Impala.

Inside, the Impala was notably safety oriented. It featured a padded bar across the instrument panel and a padded steering wheel that was contoured to the chest of the driver. The instrument panel was designed with no protruding components—all handles, levers, and switches retracted flush with the panel. A speed-warning system consisting of 10 circular windows on the instrument panel was designed to light up progressively in more intensive shades of red as higher speeds were attained.

At a time when Ford was planning to make Thunderbird a four-passenger car, there were ideas at GM to evolve the Corvette in a similar fashion. The Impala show car (sometimes referred to as the Corvette Impala) could be an indicator of what might have been if the two-seater sports car formula had been abandoned. As it turned out, the full-size sports coupe concept was designated as a model unique to Impala—just as Bel Air had the distinction of being the first Chevy hardtop—and it flourished quite nicely. The sport coupe style was immensely popular at that time, and the Impala badge was emblematic of something special from Chevrolet. Like its name suggested,

Impala was off and running, quick to leap ahead of the field and set the pace as America's favorite.

The transition from 1957 to 1958 models was the most dramatic in Chevrolet history. Many people think that because the 1957 Chevy is one of America's all-time favorite cars, it was probably the most popular car of its day. Nope. Chevrolet actually lost its perennial number one rank that year to Ford. Although it comes as a surprise to most people, it took the dramatically redesigned 1958 Chevrolet to recapture the top spot from Ford. And this was done during a model year when industry-wide sales were in the dumpster. But the evidence shows that once again America's favorite car was a Chevrolet. That point is beyond debate. It's long been said that the right product, at the right price, at the right time still adds up to success. Remember what happened to the Edsel, which was introduced this same year? Wrong product at the wrong time.

The Impala, at the top of the Chevy price line, was not substantially removed from the Edsel in price. Impala prices began under $3,000, but the car was commonly optioned out at closer to $4,000.

Impala was introduced in the same model year as Edsel, yet the results were on opposite ends of the extreme. Of course, the Impala was the king of the immensely popular Chevrolet line, while the Edsel was attempting to break new ground as a model completely separate from Ford. Yet it's an interesting comparison to notice that Chevrolet was going upscale with Impala, just as Ford was doing with Edsel. And Ford also redesigned the Thunderbird as a four-passenger personal luxury car this same year. Although many lamented the passing of the two-seat T-bird, the reality is that the bigger car was much more popular. The move may have cost Ford somewhat in terms of sporting image, but the Thunderbird image was now focused on prestige. In much the same way that the Chevy Impala was borrowing from Cadillac, the standard Ford line was borrowing from the much-celebrated Thunderbird.

The Impala was something special in 1958. It was designed to make a big splash, and included many unique features that set it apart. Most importantly, it was only available as a sport coupe and a convertible, so the sporty image was married to Impala from the beginning.

With the introduction of the Impala in 1958, Chevrolet debuted a new lineup that across the board was bigger, more luxurious, and more prestigious. Compared to the 1957 Chevy, the new models were more than 9 inches longer (2-1/2 inches in wheelbase) and 4 inches wider. Two inches were shaved from the height of the standard Chevys, but the Impala roofline was even lower, by about another inch and a

Quad headlights and quad parking lights were first used on Chevrolets in 1958. It was also the first year for the big-block engines. The 348-ci V-8 with tri-power (three two-barrel carburetors) was the hot package, and is favored by collectors. *Zone Five Photo*

A 1958 Impala convertible is a highly desirable collector car. Compared to 1957 Bel Air convertibles, they are much more rare. This onyx black example is wearing fender skirts, a distinctive accessory item. Chevrolet had a long list of accessory items, and buyers often personalized their Impalas with selections that could be ordered through the factory or the dealer. *Zone Five Photo*

Creativity was a Chevrolet styling hallmark in the late 1950s. The rear view of the 1958 Impala was suave and sophisticated. The three taillights per side was exclusive to the Impala, and except for 1959, became the Impala's signature trademark. *Zone Five Photo*

half. Chevrolets had been slowly getting longer, lower, and wider—as dictated by Harley Earl—but this was a leap.

Few people would argue that styling sells a lot more cars than engineering features, and Earl had a string of

styling successes that put GM in the forefront of automotive design. Earl liked his cars to be hefty. Size mattered to Harley Earl, who was a big, imposing man. He favored cars that were massive in appearance, and he guided Chevrolet in that direction. Earl pushed for lower rooflines and lower ground clearance. The 1958s were the last cars that truly reflected his ideas.

The design of the 1958 Impala was controversial from the beginning. That may have been a good thing because controversy gets people talking. In the case of Chevy's new luxury model, people just kept on talking and talking. Despite the much-debated styling—too conservative for some, too radical for others—the car never faltered.

Most people want to compare the 1958 and the 1957 Chevys. Although the 1957 Chevy is recognized as one of Chevy's all-time best cars, it put the 1958 at a disadvantage by virtue of its own lack of success. During the 1957 model year, Ford topped Chevy by approximately 170,000 cars in a comparison of production figures. It was the first time

Right

This Rio Red 1958 Impala sport coupe is loaded with accessories, including the continental spare tire and rear antenna seen in this photo. Notice the wraparound-style rear window that matched the wraparound windshield, and the chrome air vent (nonfunctional) centered at the rear edge of the roof. *Zone Five Photo*

Traveling the new interstate highways was a popular method of testing powerful new engine designs like the 348-ci Chevy V-8. This engine could be ordered in three different horsepower ratings: 250, 280, and 315. *Zone Five Photo*

When you sat behind the wheel of a Chevy Impala you knew you were at the controls of a special car. Attention to details created a positive impression, and factored into the pride of ownership. It was one of the things that helped create the Impala image. *Zone Five Photo*

Ford had claimed the number one position since the 1930s, and its regained momentum looked formidable going into 1958. Still, not only did Chevy reclaim the lead in 1958, it did it during a year when overall industry sales were off by almost 35 percent.

Compared to Ford, and especially to Plymouth, the Chevy design was rather blunt and boxy, and the roof was noticeably thick. In many ways it was everything the highly acclaimed Chrysler designs were not. Yet it still completed its goal of delivering an entry-level car that didn't look entry

level. The robust 1958 Impala not only led Chevy past Ford and Plymouth, but it was the key to attacking the midpriced cars and establishing new ground in the low end of the luxury field. Several months into the new car season the Chevy onslaught was in full swing.

Can a Chevy, in any shape or form, truly be considered a luxury car? Consider what it cost to buy an Impala. The convertibles were listed at a base price of $2,840. It was not uncommon, however, for buyers to load them up with options that raised the purchase price closer to $4,000—putting them well into the luxury price range. Competition was strong among GM's own divisions, and although Chevy didn't want to lose sales to Ford, it also didn't want to turn over sales to Pontiac, Olds, and Buick. GM corporate planners may have seen things differently, but the Chevrolet Division was very protective of its turf.

Much like its upscale competitors, Chevy designed the front end of the 1958 to carry a massive appearance. This was perhaps a bit of an infringement on Buick and Oldsmobile, but more importantly, it was a reflection of Harley Earl's desires. The Chevrolet budget restricted expenditures that the more expensive cars could afford, but this may have unexpectedly helped Chevy by limiting (somewhat) the ornamentation and keeping the design from going overboard.

To maintain a connection to the past, the new Chevrolet design used an extension of the 1957 grille and bumper theme. Quad headlights replaced the long-standing practice of a single headlight on each side. The quad-headlight theme was repeated with quad parking lights located in the grille opening directly below the headlights. The parking lights were tucked inside deep chrome bezels. The headlights were placed in the eyebrow portion of the fenders. When the lights were on, all four parking lights were illuminated, as well as the low-beams. When functioning as turn signals, the outermost lamp flashed.

Impala styling distinctions included two dummy extractor vents. One was centered above the back glass at the trailing edge of the coupe roof and the other, known as the pitchfork, was forward of the rear wheel openings. Fancy chrome doodads were important badges of prestige in this era, and although they are often termed excessive and unnecessary, they unquestionably added a personality and uniqueness that differentiated models and provided identification marks that owners took pride in.

The Impala interior made use of bright-colored fabrics and chrome accents on the door and instrument panels. The two-spoke, sport-style steering wheel let the man behind the wheel know he was driving something special. The back seat had the look of bucket seats, especially in the coupe where the package tray had twin humps that accentuated this effect.

Innovations abounded in the 1958 Chevrolet, and because it was the top of the line, the Impala was most often the model loaded with special options. Five years earlier Chevrolet had been a manufacturer of basic transportation,

modest a description. It was more like GM launched its own version of the space program. Its 1959 models grabbed the public's attention with the arresting commotion of a rocket launch.

Whereas the 1958 Chevrolet was more akin to a luxury yacht, the 1959 was more like a private jet. In many ways—size, weight, engine and chassis layout, and overall performance—the new cars were almost identical to the previous model. But because of all-new body dimensions and sheet metal, the perception of the new car design led to ideas that the 1959s were faster, more agile, and most importantly, more modern. It immediately dated the 1958s. Leaving them in the dust. Or worse yet, leaving them in the past. The future, Chevy wanted everyone to know, was where they were headed.

Chevrolet was still interested in building baby Cadillacs, but design ideas were changing quickly and all of General Motors, not just Chevrolet, was put on alert. A new day had come. The swanky Impala was leading the charge for the modern Chevrolet. As a 1958 model, Impala was considered a highly optioned Bel Air, available only as a hardtop coupe and a convertible. For 1959 the Impala officially replaced Bel Air as the big gun in the Chevrolet arsenal, and with that came a full series of Impala automobiles.

The story of how the 1959 Chevrolet came to be swirls around two of the most colorful characters in GM's prolific history of leaders. It takes place within an amazingly progressive era in the auto industry. And it involves an unusual juxtaposition because a manufacturer other than General Motors was suddenly setting the styling trends for car-crazy Americans.

Even though General Motors had arguably the most modern design facilities in the world, and it was staffed with the best talent money could buy, it was shocked out of its complacent security by the most forward-thinking designs of the decade. One day in 1956 the cars in the parking lot outside the Chrysler plant just down the road from the GM palace gates caught the attention of Chuck Jordan, one of General Motors' up-and-coming young designers. The cars he saw were the first of the 1957 Plymouths. They were stylishly sleek, lean, and modern. Jordan thought they were light years ahead of the completed designs he'd seen for the 1958 GM models and the plans for the GM cars of 1959. He drove back to the GM design center, loaded several other designers into his car, and returned to the Chrysler factory to show them what he was talking about. Each of them was astonished by what he saw. Back at the design center the buzz got around quickly. Bill Mitchell, Earl's first lieutenant, didn't

Impala became a series designation in 1959. In addition to the four-door sedan pictured here, the other Impala body styles included a four-door hardtop, two-door sedan, two-door coupe, and convertible. *Used with permission of GM Media Archives*

Impala buyers enjoyed a wide selection of paint and interiors in 1959. Thirteen solid colors and 10 two-tone paint schemes were available, including the Gothic Gold seen on this convertible. *1978–1999 GM Corp. Used with permission of GM Media Archives*

hesitate to make a decision: Start redesigning the 1959 models for each GM division.

For Chevrolet, or any other GM division, to be taking their styling cues from Chrysler seemed about as likely as Superman being too weak to defend "truth, justice, and the American way." But truth sometimes has a way of being stranger than fiction. And when a few of the influential designers at GM saw what Chrysler was doing with the "Forward Look" for 1957, they realized the trouble they were in. They also realized the opportunity it presented.

The design of the 1959 Chevy was well under way when GM got its wake-up call. Long before this, however, the corporate planners had decided on a plan that would bring big changes to Chevrolet design for the 1959 model year. Chevy, Pontiac, Oldsmobile, and Buick agreed to

reduce costs by implementing a body-sharing program. Each division would begin with the same body structure in order to take advantage of volume purchases and shared tooling for under-the-surface materials. Naturally each division would still do its own body design and create its own brand of automobile. The inter-division agreement meant Chevrolet would realize another growth spurt in 1959. It played right into the baby Cadillac idea and the Harley Earl dogma: longer, lower, wider.

Planning for this bigger, more luxurious version of the 1958 Chevy was under way when Mitchell made the decision that a clean sheet of paper needed to be brought out of the drawer. To substantially change design ideas in midstream was a bold move. It would not only put incredible pressure on the design staff to come up with new ideas within the confines of strict deadlines, but the change in direction would have to be approved by Harley Earl, one of the most powerful and imposing executives in GM's storied history. Earl was in Europe when it became clear that changes must be implemented.

Earl could have stopped such talk in less time than it would take a flyswatter to smack the life out of a fly, but rather than dig in his heels, he went along with the sea change of new ideas that had quickly begun to swell. Perhaps he was willing to trust and place the responsibility in the hands of his hand-picked successor, Bill Mitchell. Earl was on the verge of retirement. Perhaps he saw the exciting possibilities presented by the Chrysler ideas. Or perhaps he noticed the newfound enthusiasm exuding from the younger designers. They were eager to go down new roads and regain the role of design leadership in the auto industry. Whatever it was, Earl recognized the time had come for change. He had personally led the Motorama dream car projects through the 1950s. Implementing some of the imagination that he had cultivated for years was probably not an obstacle for Harley Earl. He would play a major role in the development of the most creative process that was ever played out in the American car industry. "Go as far as you can with your design ideas," he was known to say. "I'll let you know if you go too far."

The 1959 Impalas, some say, are too bizarre, too unconventional, too . . . extreme. Everyone had (and continues to have) an opinion about this car and—as generally is the case—those who dislike something make the most noise. The most severe criticism came several years into the 1960s after the auto industry became much more conser-vative, and all the cars of the late 1950s seemed cartoonish in comparison. Those critiques seemed to have stuck with the 1959 forever.

But there are a couple of things to take into consideration. In 1959 this car was nothing short of a sales success. It proved to be exciting then, and even now it is one of the most easily recognized and talked about Chevrolets of all time. In retrospect, this car was perfect for the times. It's also important to note that collectors love this car. And people who see it today are quickly impressed with its out-going personality.

One thing is for certain: The 1959 Impala did not suffer from an identity crisis. It wasn't a car that simply blended into the crowd. Its most notable feature was the startling, horizontal rear fins, sometimes referred to as gullwings or batwings. Fins, in 1959, were in. They were stylish. And, yes, you can say it, size mattered. Why have fins at all if they are just going to be small? Earlier in the decade nearly every manufacturer had a fin of some stature. But just when everyone was expecting fins to grow taller, Chevrolet developed its own distinctive fash-ion statement. And rather than placing a lantern-style tail-light in a tall fin, Chevy placed a "cat's eye" taillight lens below its wing-like fin. It was daring. And it made a state-ment that Chevy was marching to the beat of its own drummer. Chevy deserves credit for not dancing to some-one else's music.

There were many styling trends developed in the 1959 that were overshadowed by talk of whether the fins were appropriate or not. The headlights, for instance, were no longer positioned in the tops of fenders, as was the industry

The four-door hardtop featured a unique roof design that was referred to as the flat top. Like the sport coupe, it featured ultrathin roof pillars and offered great visibility. Visually the 1959 Impala appeared to be a much lighter car than the 1958, but in actuality the overall weight was almost identical. *1978–1999 GM Corp. Used with permission of GM Media Archives*

Interior design elements included a glovebox door designed with cup holders—a thoughtful convenience when visiting the drive-in diner. Another practical idea was the flat area on the dashboard where items could be laid out without falling off. One of the many accessory items was a vacuum ashtray that sucked away cigarette ashes to a receptacle stashed inside the engine compartment. *Late Great Chevy Collection*

standard for years. This was the first year they were incorporated into the grille area, a move that was copied by competitors and quickly became the new standard. The roof designs on the coupes and sedans were amazing engineering accomplishments and beautifully styled. In some models the glass area was increased by 50 percent. The bumpers were completely redesigned to make them lighter, less cumber-

some, and far more modern. And the hood was redesigned, too, to make it lower and flatter while providing a visual cue that this car was wider, roomier, and more streamlined than the previous model.

The fact that this design was sailing in uncharted waters never diminished confidence that the job could be done nor dampened the imagination that pushed these

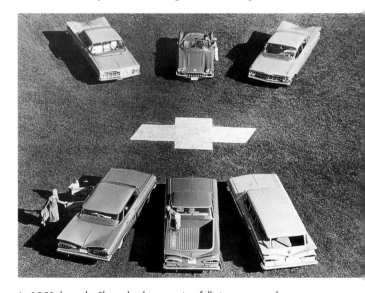

The big-block 348-ci engine was back for its second year. In marketing lingo it was referred to as the Turbo-Thrust. It was available in six horsepower ratings from 250 to 335, and each had its own name. The four-barrel version (seen here) featured a high-lift cam and 11.25:1 compression. It was rated at 320 horsepower and was called the Special Turbo-Thrust. *1978–1999 GM Corp. Late Great Chevy Collection*

In 1959 the only Chevrolet that wasn't a full-size car was the Corvette. This Chevy family photo includes the El Camino and the station wagon. Both were built on the same full-size Chevy chassis as the Impala, but neither was afforded the extra features that made the Impala a distinctive model. *Late Great Chevy Collection*

Options & Accessories for your Chevy Impala

Factory options:
Air conditioning
Air suspension
Positraction
Heavy-duty battery
Dual exhaust
Temperature-controlled radiator fan
35-, 40-, & 50-amp generators
Tinted glass
Shaded rear window
Heater/defroster: DeLuxe, outside air;
    Recirculating, inside air
Radio, manual or push-button;
    select front or rear antenna
Power brakes
Power steering
Power windows
Power seats
Heavy-duty coil springs
Wheel discs
Two-speed wipers and washers

Dealer-installed accessories:
Dummy left rear antenna
Autronic eye
Seat belt
Locking gas cap
Continental spare
    (one-piece bumper and three-piece bumper)
Luggage carrier
Electric clock
Illuminated compass

Litter container
Accelerator pedal cover
Full wheel covers
Tissue dispenser
Glareshades for windshield and rear window
DeLuxe license frame
Door-edge guards
Front bumper grille guard
Shoulder harness seatbelts
Luggage compartment lamp
Underhood lamp
Courtesy lamps (not available on convertible)
Glove compartment lamps
Ashtray lamp
Floor mats
Inside and outside rearview mirrors
Vanity visor-mirror
Body sill molding
Front fender ornaments
Port exhaust
Safety light
Radiator insect screen
Door handle shield
Parking brake warning signal
Rear-seat radio speaker
Spinner hub caps and wheel covers
Speedminder
Portable hand-held spotlight
Outside-mounted spotlight
Vacuum ashtray
Ventshades
Throttle holder

ideas forward into reality. What seems most incredible in today's world is that an automobile company was daring enough to take this on. That General Motors and Chevrolet had the fortitude to see the importance of this task and to go out and get it done is remarkable. And it was accomplished within strict time constraints, under unusually tight deadlines.

In its second year as the top Chevrolet, the Impala series included two-door hardtops (sport coupes), convertibles, four-door sedans, and four-door hardtops (sport sedans). The sport coupes (172,000 built) and convertibles (72,000 built) were exclusive to the Impala line. The sedan body styles were shared with Bel Air and Biscayne.

While Impala settled into its role as the most glamorous Chevrolet, Bel Air was demoted to second-best status. The Bel Air's accomplishments during the 1950s, which set the table for Impala, were yesterday's news. The Bel Air name was closely tied to the past, and not just past success. It was also a part of the six-cylinder past, and that wouldn't do for the luxuriously appointed future. A new and exciting nameplate was needed to lead the way. And that honor would go to Impala. History would repeat itself in the years ahead, when Impala would eventually fall victim to the same plan for modernization. As Bel Air slipped a notch in terms of status, the Biscayne did the same—becoming the entry-level Chevrolet. This left no room for the Del Ray model, and that name was retired.

Impala interiors could not match the fanciful array of materials, paint, and chrome that were used in 1958, but that's not to say they weren't exciting or colorful. Just the

The sport coupe body style was an Impala exclusive in 1959. It was 2 inches lower than the Bel Air and Biscayne two-door sedans. Accentuating the length of the car was a side molding that almost connected the headlights to the taillight. It, too, was unique to the Impala. *1978–1999 GM Corp. Used with permission of GM Media Archives*

Tri-power carburetion on the 348 was referred to as the Special Super Turbo-Thrust engine. It could be ordered with 11.25:1 compression, which was rated at 335 horsepower or with 11:1 compression, which was rated at 315 horsepower. Both versions came with a special high-lift cam. *Zone Five Photo*

opposite was true. Interior design was a highlight for Impala. It played an important role in the success of the car. Coupes and sedans featured a combination cloth and vinyl upholstery done in three colors. The inside door panels were highly styled and the armrest/door handle was integrated for convenience. Notable for their ease of operation were the paddle-style door handles. And the armrests featured reflectors that provided a measure of safety when the doors were opening into a lane of traffic at night. The front seats were dressed up with a bright anodized aluminum end panel that also provided protection to an area that generally becomes tattered and worn.

The five-pod instrument panel design—a carryover from the classic 1957 Chevy—featured gauges that were deep set to prevent glare. Impalas had their own sport-style steering wheel design that was better looking than anyone else's; it was an important aspect of exclusivity and owner satisfaction. Across the entire instrument panel was a bright anodized aluminum trim piece that also added character to the overall appearance. Above the glovebox in front of the passenger, the dash was flat so that miscellaneous items (cheeseburgers and fries) could be conveniently laid there without falling off or rolling down the defroster vents. (I hate it when fries roll into the defroster vents.) When the

Impala interiors offered as standard equipment anodized aluminum trim molding, the Impala nameplate, an electric clock, a parking brake alarm, a deep-hub steering wheel with perforated spokes and half-circle horn ring, a rear-seat speaker grille, dual side-rail interior lights (except on convertibles), aluminum seat-end panels, carpet, and bright-metal moldings around the windshield and rear window, side roof rails (coupes and sedans), and door trim. *Zone Five Photo*

For 1959, Chevy convertibles were only produced in the Impala line, with total production reaching 72,765. Base price for the Impala convertible was $2,967, but most were ordered with enough optional equipment to raise the price another $1,000. *Zone Five Photo*

Most of the trim on the 1959 Impala, including the strip down the center of the deck lid, was made of stainless steel. The stainless pieces held up well over the years, making restoration of these items much easier than those made of anodized aluminum. *Zone Five Photo*

glovebox door was opened, it doubled as a tray where drinks from the drive-in restaurant could be placed. Not quite a cup holder, but a thoughtful convenience item nonetheless.

Stainless-steel trim pieces covered the windshield pillars, across the top of the windshield, along the side rails, and around the rear window. And the sport coupes featured a cosmic-looking headliner that twinkled like a starry night. This was an interior with a lot of personality. It also was an interior with a lot of metal, which would be replaced with plastics in the near future.

On the exterior of the Impala, as well, stainless-steel trim was used liberally. Window reveal molding was entirely stainless steel. The trim that outlined the fins and passed through the center of the deck lid was also stainless. Additional Impala-only brightwork included the anodized aluminum side trim spear, the bezels that set off the cat's eye taillights and divided the taillight lenses into sections, the headlight bezels, parking light bezels, air inlet frames and screens, and the entire grille body and screen.

A new acrylic lacquer that GM called "Magic Mirror" was used for the first time on the 1959s. It was said to pro-

Chevrolet advertising noted the fine-car attributes of the Impala, inviting comparisons with more expensive cars. Base price of the two-door sport coupe with a 283-ci V-8 engine was $2,717.

vide a deeper, richer color saturation. Thirteen single-color paint options and 10 two-tone paint options were available to choose from.

While so much was developing on the exterior and interior of the 1959 Chevy, the mechanicals—engine and chassis—were essentially unchanged from the previous year. The popularity of the six-cylinder engine seemed endless, but the two-year-old 283 V-8 was gaining a lot of converts. In its mildest form, the 283 could be almost as economical and practical as the highly respected six, which was still undeniably tied to the Chevrolet tradition. But this classic small block had an inordinate potential for power.

The fuel-injected 283 of this era was a heroic attempt to develop high performance. Although more commonly seen on the 1957 Chevy Bel Air and the Corvettes from 1957 to 1965, this remarkable engine did make a surprise appearance under the hood of a few 1959 full-size Chevys. It was the final year this engine could be ordered in any car other than the Corvette.

The big-block 348, in its second year of production, was also picking up customers. It was clear that the Impala's luxury and performance image relied on the 348 for much of its luster. The most common 348s were the 250- and 280-horsepower versions that operated on 9.5:1 compression. The 280-horse engine made use of the tri-power (three two-barrel carbs) system, an optional item that collectors love. There were three 348s that cranked out more than 300 horsepower by adding high-lift cams and 11:1 compression. The big dog, at 320 horsepower, took compression to 11.25:1 and used a single four-barrel carb. The enormous 348s were a tight fit into the engine compartments of the 1959s and 1960s.

The Inside Story on Fuel Injected 283s

The Ramjet fuel injection was available in two "street" versions of the 283-ci engines. One was calibrated for use with the 250-horsepower engine that used hydraulic lifters, the standard camshaft, 9.5:1 compression, and torque output rated at 305 foot-pounds. The other was calibrated for the highly publicized 283-horsepower engine that used solid lifters. There was also a third version, which was a racing fuelie. It, too, was "officially" listed at 283 horsepower, but was known to exceed 300 horses.

Three elements make up the fuel injection system: a unique aluminum intake manifold, the air meter, and a fuel meter–injector nozzle assembly. A high-pressure fuel pump, driven by the distributor, delivered the gas.

For guys used to tinkering with carburetors, fuel injection was a finicky beast. Many of the fuelies were snatched up by high-performance enthusiasts who worked on their own cars, but had no experience with the fuel-injection system. The FI systems were rare and those who really knew how to work on them were even more rare.

The air-to-fuel ratio was strictly calibrated and an overzealous or inexperienced mechanic could easily make misadjustments. If the calibration was altered, there was no way to recalibrate units in the field. The only answer was to replace the fuel meter and nozzle set with a new or factory recalibrated unit.

Maintenance was critical and replacement of fuel- and air-filter elements was vitally important. Idle-speed and mixture adjustments were normally unnecessary unless the unit was being rebuilt.

According to the shop manual, extreme care is necessary when cleaning fuel-injection parts. Minuscule amounts of dirt, a problem in any fuel system, brought serious consequences to the fuel-injection unit because of the close tolerances and tiny orifices. Fuel cleanliness was also critical to operating efficiency. Cheap gasoline, which leads to a buildup of gum and varnish, could decimate an FI system.

The shop manual advised mechanics to thoroughly check the engine and ignition systems before attacking the fuel injection. Troubleshooting such problems as hard starting, hesitation, rough idling, and flat spots in acceleration began with checks of other fuel-related areas and often led to solutions that were not the fault of the widely misunderstood fuel injection.

Some likely areas of trouble included air leaks at the signal line connections and nozzle blocks, or leaks in the enrichment or main control diaphragms.

Improvements were made to the earliest Ramjets, but the word got around that the system wasn't worth the trouble. Eventually common problems were corrected: stabilized idle, better hot starting capability, better partial throttle "tip-in" performance, and improved fuel economy.

CHAPTER 3

Moving into the Passing Lane

"The law of competition...is best for the race, because it ensures the survival of the fittest in every department."

—*Andrew Carnegie*

An often-heard criticism lobbed at the 1959 Chevrolet was that it was too extreme. Without question it roused a response from nearly everyone—people either loved it or hated it. Few were unfazed. But take into consideration that the new Chevrolet, and all automobile design for this era, was unbound by tradition. Opinions that counted the most, those that led to a purchase, once again determined Chevrolet to be America's most-liked car. And the Chevrolet in the spotlight most often was the Impala. So much for the idea that it was too extreme to be popular.

Instead of an all-new Chevy—as there was in 1958 and 1959—the 1960 Chevys remained true to the previous year's model, while incorporating subtle changes. In traditional fashion, the most flamboyant design elements of the 1959 were softened to become more conventional. (Keep in mind that this was done in advance of the 1959 ever being seen by the public.) At the center of this

More people bought convertible Impalas in 1960 than in either of the previous years. This Tuxedo Black model is equipped with stylish accessories such as fender skirts, door handle shields, front fender ornaments, body sill moldings, and dual rear antennae. *Zone Five Photo*

Overall styling of the 1960 Impala was less flamboyant. Side trim was highlighted by a stylized jet, and did not stretch the entire length of the car as it had the year before. The sport sedan remained a popular body style that outsold sport coupes. *1978–1999 GM Corp. Used with permission of GM Media Archives*

redesign focus were the much-talked-about gullwing fins and taillight treatment.

Fins were losing their fashion appeal. They had been around in one form or another since Harley Earl introduced them on the 1947 Cadillac. For more than a dozen years, they were used in various shapes and sizes and placed at different angles. Claims of excessiveness (think of the Oldsmobiles, DeSotos, and Edsels of 1958) were—to some degree—tarnishing the industry at this time. Heavy chrome and appliqués were public enemies number one and two. So the wild exuberance of the 1959 fins gave way to a more buttoned-down restraint in 1960. All Chevrolets shared this treatment.

In a move that was special for the Impala, the taillights returned to the round, bullet-shaped, six-across style. When introduced in 1958, the Impala was the only

Chevrolet with this feature, and in time this would become an instantly recognizable trademark. In 1959 all Chevys displayed the distinctive cat's-eye taillight. It provided a ready identification for Chevy, but the Impala had no distinction over the others. Impala, for 1960, once again enjoyed the taillight status symbol of three round lamps per side, while the Bel Air and Biscayne had to settle for two per side, or a total of four.

Up front the grille was a more traditional horizontal bar design, and the "eyebrow" vents at the leading edge of the hood were eliminated. The quad headlights, which were separate from the grille but placed within their own anodized aluminum elements in 1959, were incorporated into the grille treatment. This, combined with the horizontal bars of the grille and the removal of the eyebrow vents, created a front-end design that was more integrated and

The three taillights per side configuration replaced the one-year-only cat's eye lenses from 1959, and the gullwing fins were toned down considerably. As in 1959, the gasoline filler spout was hidden behind the license plate. *1978–1999 GM Corp. Used with permission of GM Media Archives*

Without the nostrils—the slit-like vents above the grille in the 1959—the 1960 Chevy appears more normal. People either love or hate the 1959, but remain more neutral on the 1960. The headlights are more naturally integrated into the grille without the separate pods that contained them in 1959. *Zone Five Photo*

seemed wider. The entire grille was outlined with anodized aluminum trim, and spears wrapped around the front fenders from the midpoint of the headlights to the top edge of the front wheelwell.

The side trim that had the appearance of a spear on the 1959 Impala (similar to the 1958) was replaced by a less cumbersome trim that featured two narrow bands of anodized aluminum streaming from the wing tips of a stylized aircraft made of stainless steel. The nose of the aircraft was positioned slightly behind the midpoint of the car—reaching the front door in two-door models, but not quite making it that far on the four-door models—and the twin trim pieces framed a white-painted inset area on all cars (except white cars, which had the inset painted black). The leaping Impala and crossed-flags badge was positioned just behind the jet emblem.

Not only was this side trim more proportional to the overall design of the car, it was a one-year deviation from the full body-length side molding that was traditionally found on Chevrolets. A visual line from the top of the front

Magazine advertisements for the 1960 Chevrolet carried the message that Impala offered more luxury than was previously available in any low-priced car. The combination of luxury and economy was the basis for the Impala's escalating success.

Both the 1959 and 1960 Impalas had huge trunks capable of devouring the luggage requirements of the typical family on vacation. A ribbed, anodized aluminum cove trim surrounded the taillights and added interesting detail to the rear of the Impala. *Zone Five Photo*

fender to the top of the rear fender was still apparent—a recurring theme for Chevrolet and a styling trick to make a car appear longer. The preponderance of brightwork, however, was reduced by only carrying it through two-thirds of the length. In 1961, and for three years thereafter, full-length brightwork returned.

Anodized aluminum continued to replace chrome plating on an industry-wide basis. And on the Chevrolets, it was the Impala that wore more of it than the other models. For 1960 it provided a degree of luster to distinctively Impala features such as the grille, the headlight bezels, and the cove panels that surrounded the taillights.

This was the era when the options list for an automobile was longer than the walk from the parking lot to the salesman's office. As the status-maker of the Chevrolet line, the Impalas naturally offered more features as standard equipment than the less expensive Bel Airs and Biscaynes. The distinctions were apparent with more chrome trim inside and out, a wider selection of colors, and finer interior fabrics. But that was just the tip of the options list. To begin with, there were six engines, and two manual and two automatic transmissions. By doing the math, you'd find a total of 24 engine/transmission combinations. Then the assortment of rear axle ratios was added into the mix.

The standard Impala engine for 1960 was the 283-ci V-8. Since its introduction in 1957, the 283 had developed a loyal following as Chevy fanatics traded in their old six-cylinder cars for this V-8. It was immensely popular, especially with the two-barrel carburetor and 8.5:1 compression ratio that was rated at 170 horsepower. With the four-barrel carb and 9.5:1 compression, the horsepower rating climbed to 230. The aftermarket performance parts businesses made this engine their darling, and that turned out to be the kiss of good fortune. The 283 benefited from a high-performance street and strip reputation, and was highly regarded for dependability and economy in the family garage.

For the economy minded, and those who believed a Chevrolet should forever be powered with an inline six, there was the steadfast and true, direct descendent of the 30-year-old "Stove-bolt Six."

But the sweet seduction of a powerful V-8 had the greatest allure. The construction of super highways, the availability of cheap fuel, and the almost insatiable desire to travel put big V-8s in demand. In the Chevrolet line, those who wanted a more potent option that would run faster and power more accessories could choose from a combo of 348-ci engines that delivered a big dose of muscle—from a minimum of 250 horsepower with a four-barrel carb and 8.5:1 compression, up to 335 horsepower with the tri-power carburetion, a high-lift cam, 11.25:1 compression, mechanical lifters, and dual exhaust.

What you were running was identified by badges. In later years these badges included the cubic-inch displacement within the badge, but in this era things were more subtle. You learned to read the signs. For instance, cars

The two-door hardtop body style—the sport coupe—was no longer an Impala exclusive in 1960, as Bel Air shared in the increasing popularity of this pretty car. Notice how the windshield and rear window glass curve upward into the roof. *1978–1999 GM Corp. Used with permission of GM Media Archives*

New to the Impala lineup in 1961 was a two-door sedan body style. Other Impala body styles included the four-door sedan, four-door sport sedan, two-door convertible, and two-door sport coupe. Although more than twice as many sedans were sold, the Impala image was tied to the sport coupe and convertible. *1978–1999 GM Corp. Used with permission of GM Media Archives*

packing a 283 wore a Chevy crest and *V* on both the hood and rear deck lid. The badge for cars powered by the big 348 engine was a *V* with crossed flags. Six-cylinder cars used Chevy emblems without the *V*.

The fuel-injected 283-ci engines, which had been produced in limited numbers beginning with the 1957s, were no longer an option in the full-size Chevrolets, but a few are known to have made their way into 1960 models. The 348 engines, introduced in the 1958 Chevrolet, were on the verge of extinction. An even more powerful replacement was on the horizon.

Available with all engine options in 1960 were transmission and gear ratios that could be mixed and matched

to tailor the car to the owner's driving style. Scared-rabbit acceleration, highway-cruising performance, fuel economy, and manual or automatic shifting preferences could be dialed in. With engines over 290 horsepower, Chevy preferred you use a manual transmission. If you wanted an automatic transmission, you had to take the old Powerglide and a 305-horse 348. That transmission used 3.55 gears, so performance was strong. Three-speed manual transmissions could match up with any engine, but four-speeds were reserved for the engines over 250 horsepower. A four-speed car got the 3.70 gears, as did a three-speed if the horsepower topped 320. With this combination and an aggressive tendency behind the wheel, the screech of burning rubber

Because of the bulge in the rear window glass of the sport coupe, that body style gained the nickname "bubble top." Sedans continued with the flat-roof design similar to 1959 and 1960. *1978–1999 GM Corp. Used with permission of GM Media Archives*

Without the fins that were a big part of the Chevrolet identity in 1959 and 1960, the 1961 Chevy seemed like a completely different car. However, the rooflines and the glass area were carryovers from the 1959 and 1960 cars. *1978–1999 GM Corp. Used with permission of GM Media Archives*

Overall, the 1961s were noticeably squared off at the edge of the trunk, with sheet-metal contours that resembled the fins from 1960. The six cone-shaped taillights carried over from 1958 and 1960, and by this time nearly everyone knew an Impala when they saw one. *1978–1999 GM Corp. Used with permission of GM Media Archives*

was almost unavoidable. (So were the grins.) Those 3.70 gears were also used in the six-cylinder cars with three-speed transmissions (typically ordered with overdrive transmissions). A three-speed manual when matched up with a 280-horsepower (or less) engine took the 3.36 gears.

In 1960 the tried-and-true, two-speed Powerglide was Chevy's most popular transmission. It wasn't fast and it

wasn't smooth, but it was sure popular. Its gear ratio was 3.08, so it was the rational choice for most driving habits. The Turboglide automatic was an option, but not a very good one, and Chevy didn't use it in the six-cylinder cars or with the two top-performing engines.

Chevrolet owners continued to migrate toward the Impala model. Traditionally Chevrolet represented low-

The rake and contour of the 1961 Impala convertible windshield is evident in this photo. The curvature of the windshield A-pillar necessitated a teardrop-shaped vent window. *1978–1999 GM Corp. Used with permission of GM Media Archives*

priced value, and the least expensive Chevys usually sold best. This was still true in 1960, but the popularity of the Impala was an indication of things to come. Chevy relied on the six-cylinder engine until 1955, and many of its loyal customers remained true to the six-cylinders for many years after. But the success of the Impala signaled a change in desire. Chevrolet had a strong brand image, and those who didn't want to switch brands still wanted to move up to a higher-quality car. Impala was the answer. Fancier trim and upholstery, more options such as power steering and power brakes, a V-8 or even a big V-8 were increasingly popular. The Impala changed the image of Chevrolet. Luxury and power were its promise. Of course, there had always been a top-of-the-line Chevrolet, but the Impala was the right car for America at a perfect time. Two-car families were becoming more common, and the youth market was a much bigger factor in new-car sales.

In the 10 years between 1950 and 1960, Chevrolets—as well as most every other car made in the United States—grew considerably. The traditional small cars—Chevy, Ford, and Plymouth—were in a race to reinvent themselves in the likeness of the luxury marques. By 1960 these low-priced cars left room for a new class of economical small cars to carve a new market niche. Each of the Big Three manufacturers saw this coming and prepared new compact models to fit into this slot. Up to this point, Chevy (and its direct competitors) had a one-size-fits-all approach to building cars. That idea changed forever in 1960 with the introduction of the compacts. Within the Chevrolet ranks, the Impala, Bel Air, and Biscayne shared sales with the newcomer, Corvair.

The Corvair, Ford Falcon, and Plymouth Valiant ushered in the age of automotive diversification. Soon there would be an onslaught of models to fit the niche markets

1960 Chevrolet Engine Specifications

High Thrift	6 cyl 235-ci	single-bbl carb	8.25:1 compression	135 hp
Turbo-Fire	V-8 283-ci	two-bbl carb	8.5:1 compression	170 hp
Super Turbo-Fire	V-8 283-ci	four-bbl carb	9.5:1 compression	230 hp
Turbo-Thrust	V-8 348-ci	four-bbl carb	9.5:1 compression	250 hp
Super Turbo-Thrust	V-8 348-ci	tri-power carb	9.5:1 compression	280 hp
Special Turbo-Thrust	V-8 348-ci	tri-power carb	11:1 compression	305 hp
*Special Turbo-Thrust	V-8 348-ci	four-bbl carb	11:25 compression	320 hp
*Special Super Turbo-Thrust	V-8 348-ci	tri-power carb	11:25 compression	335 hp

*Special Turbo-Thrust and Special Super Turbo-Thrust engines included a high-lift cam and mechanical lifters in their bag of high-performance tricks.

The front-end design indicated this Impala was ready for the 1960s. The grille returned to the more traditional egg-crate style. *Zone Five Photo*

that were flourishing in the absence of a low-priced full-size car. The advent of the Corvair may not have had a great effect on Impala sales, but as the 1960s rolled forward Chevrolet buyers would have many more new-car purchasing choices. Each would play a role in deflecting attention away from the singular spotlight that Impala once enjoyed. In its first year of production the Corvair sold 250,000 cars.

In the big car lineup, convertibles were once again exclusive to the Impala, an indication of Impala's prestigious place in the Chevy brand. Sales reached nearly 80,000 units, an increase of about 8,000 from the year

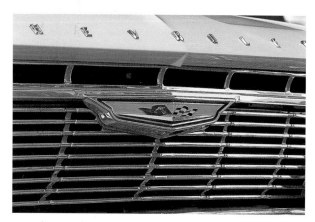

As in the past, the crossed-flags emblem—this time in the top center of the grille—indicated a 348 engine was under the hood. About mid-1961 the 348 was phased out when the famed 409 muscled its way onto the scene. *Zone Five Photo*

before. The sport coupe, previously an Impala-only option, was shared with Bel Air. The popularity of the sport coupe style was rising faster than the water temperature in a flathead Ford. So making it affordable to more people made sense.

Sport sedans, the four-door hardtops, were once again available in either Impala or Bel Air trim. But the sport sedan sales dropped, as did sales for both two- and four-door sedans. Regardless of that trend, four-door sedans remained twice as popular as the next-most-asked-for body style—the two-door sedan. In 1960 those figures reached nearly 500,000 (Impalas, Bel Airs, and Bicaynes) four-door sedans and more than 228,000 two-door sedans (Bel Airs and Biscaynes only).

An Impala could provide many, if not all, the same things as a Pontiac, a Buick, an Oldsmobile, and even a Cadillac. The grand plan of General Motors—to move buyers from a Chevy to a Pontiac to a Buick and so forth—was sidetracked due to customer brand loyalty and a competition among the divisions that wasn't conducive to handing over customers to the next highest division on the status scale. The Impala provided status for Chevrolet and, more importantly, for the Chevrolet owner. A nice house and a great-looking Chevrolet in the driveway were plenty good enough for many Americans.

Inside an Impala the attention to design details made this Chevrolet special, and in many owners' minds as good as more expensive automobiles. For instance, it was the only model that offered patterned cloth seats in a style that was associated with more expensive, more glamorous cars. These fabric seat covers were only used on the closed cars, while the convertibles used a more durable patterned vinyl. A stylish, textured vinyl headliner was another extra that was a standard Impala feature. It added a degree of sex appeal that set Impala apart from the rest of the field. Plain cloth was the old and unimaginative way to trim the interior. Deep-pile, wall-to-wall carpet was also an Impala exclusive within the Chevy model range.

Standard features also included an electric clock, a parking-brake alarm, a deep-hub steering wheel with perforated spokes and a half-circle horn ring, a rear-seat radio speaker grille, dual side-rail interior lights rather than the single center-mounted dome light, aluminum seat-end panels, and bright-metal moldings above and on the sides of the windshield and rear window, side roof rails, and door trim. Don't forget the Impala nameplate on the instrument panel.

1961 Impala: Good Times Getting Better

Now in its fourth year on the road, the Impala name had quickly become synonymous with style, performance, quality, and value. The top-of-the-line full-size Ford, the Galaxie, and Plymouth's equivalent, the Fury, were successful, but both were left in the huge shadow of the popular Impala.

It would be a decade ruled from beginning to end by the Impala—no other car came close to matching its widespread popularity.

A new era in Impala history began with the introduction of the 1961 Chevrolet. For the third time in four years, there was a redesigned Chevy in the showrooms. Whereas the 1960 Impala was linked to the 1950s, the latest version set the stage for the 1960s.

With the influence of Harley Earl now a historical reference point, the GM design took on a renewed vigor under the direction of Bill Mitchell. Mitchell was Earl's hand-picked successor, and he gave considerable credit to Earl for influencing his management approach and view toward overall corporate design, but Mitchell was very much his own man. Like Earl, he fully believed he knew best when it came to design, and he ruled the design studios with an iron fist. Although he clearly had his own ideas, he tailored them to the degree necessary for preserving the corporate image of the individual marques.

The Chevys of 1957, 1958, and 1959 bore little resemblance to one another. On one hand, these annual introductions were a sign of Chevrolet's leadership and boldness to step confidently into the future. These were, after all, heady times in America. New space-age technologies were leading industry to new products and new conveniences. Commercial air travel surged as jets took the place of slower propeller planes. The superhighways had a similar impact on ground transportation. Prosperity provided many more people with the means to have more and do more. The fact that Chevrolet was introducing new products at such a rapid pace bolstered its image as a leader and an innovator. It was an excellent time to fly fast and high, and Impala was out front.

Trimmings

As the flagship of the Chevrolet line of full-size cars, Impalas received the greatest amount of brightwork. Anodized aluminum, stainless steel, and chrome plating were extensively used to distinguish the model hierarchy. Although not as "dressed-up" as the original Impala of 1958, the Impalas of the early 1960s still flashed a variety of ornamentation. The use of aluminum was increasing because it could be stamped rather than diecast, a cost-saving as well as a weight-saving measure. As the cars aged, the aluminum used on the exterior lost its luster; therefore, finding a car of this vintage with still-shiny aluminum trim is rare. Conversely, the stainless-steel trim that was used held up exceedingly well, and the original 40-year-old trim pieces can often be polished to look as good as new.

1960 Impala
Anodized aluminum trim parts:
Grille, including the frame and emblem bezel
Headlight frames
Taillight frames
Radiator grille extensions and bars
Rear-end trim plate
Backup light frames
Rear-end panel molding
Series ornaments

Stainless-steel trim parts:
Windshield frame
Deck lid edge molding
Series ornament
Belt molding
Roof moldings
Rear quarter window reveal

Chrome-plated trim parts:
Bumpers
Twin vertical guards on front and rear bumpers
Nameplate on hood
Door handles

Factory Amenities

The standard Impala was equipped with many of the same types of upgrades as all top-of-the-line Chevrolets before it. Certain items—such as extra chrome and stainless steel trim both outside and in, nicer wheel covers, plusher and more colorful interior fabrics, and badges that signified a difference between this car and other Chevrolets—were always part of the option list. However, the options and accessories list had grown considerably by 1960. For instance, not only was there air conditioning, there were two options. The deluxe A/C included a heavy-duty radiator and a temperature-controlled radiator fan and heater. It was only available in cars with automatic transmissions. The regular A/C, without the extras, was labeled Cool Pack. Air conditioning was still in its early years of development, and was a rare option on Chevrolets. However, tinted glass was gaining in popularity. It could be ordered on all the windows, or just on the windshield or just on the rear window.

A new item for 1960 was the automatic headlight beam control called Guide-Matic. It dimmed the bright lights when traffic approached. Radios were available with or without push-buttons, and the antenna placement—front or rear—could be selected. Standard windshield wipers were one-speed only, but the two-speed version was an option.

Power accessories—items once reserved for luxury automobiles—were increasingly ordered as options on Chevrolets, and especially on Impalas. These included power brakes, power steering, power windows, and power seats. In addition to the various engine and transmission options, items such as Posi-Traction (a limited-slip differential that directed power to the rear wheel with the most traction), heavy-duty shocks, and heavy-duty coil springs were popular with those who put their cars through more difficult paces.

Accessory items were extremely popular. There were many ways to add gadgets, flashy trim, and safety features not available on the assembly line cars. These were dealer installed accessories, and they offered a high degree of personalization similar to having a custom-built car.

Sporty cars of this era had radio antennas mounted on the right rear fender. They could be ordered that way from the factory. But for that extra degree of coolness, a dummy antenna could be installed on the left rear fender. Another sporty appearance item was the chrome-plated accelerator pedal cover. Door-edge guards, door-handle shields, front and rear bumper guards, body sill molding, front fender ornaments, and fake port exhausts in the rear quarter panels were also available to dress up an Impala.

Under the category of safety features there were four-way hazard flashers, a rear-window defroster, lap-style seat belts, and an adjustable excessive-speed warning device called Speedminder.

Other conveniences included cruise control, illuminated compass, courtesy lamps in the luggage compartment and the ashtray, and even a vacuum-suction ashtray that whisked ashes to a container in the engine compartment.

The flip side of these product changes was a diminished familiarity and continuity. Mitchell and the GM design team began a process of restoring that continuity—that strong Chevy brand image—with the plans for the 1961 models. Design work on the 1961 models was developed and approved during 1958 and 1959. And although the goal was to move into a new generation of cars, the steps taken were far less extreme.

There would be some important characteristics to provide a bridge to the past. By this time it was clearly established that the Impala identity was strongly tied to the visually distinctive six round taillights. The establishment of rank by taillight configuration had been well received during the Impala's premier year of 1958, and the soon-to-be-released 1960 Impala would use this feature as well.

Rather than continue the 1950s battle of who could design the most flamboyant fins, Chevy set its sights on the future, figuring finless was the best way to step out of the past and away from the competition. It was time to move on.

But rather than ignoring the previous design, the rear sheet metal and bright trim traced an outline clearly reminiscent of the 1960's swoopy style. It moved ahead, but didn't lose sight of the past. The rear-end design was far more simple than before, slightly boxy and more conservative in appearance. The bullet-shaped triple taillights on each side played an even more prominent role. As in 1958, the taillights were unadorned. On the 1960 design, Impalas featured an anodized aluminum trim panel that surrounded the taillights. The trim panel was one of the Impala exclusives, and made the rear-end design more attractive

Vertical bumper guards, as seen on this convertible, provided only a small amount of protection for the rear taillights, but they looked good. The popularity of wide whitewall tires was reaching its end. *Zone Five Photo*

With a bit of imagination and sunlight from the proper angle, it's not difficult to imagine this car still has fins. Full-length side molding returned after a one-year absence. *Zone Five Photo*

compared to the more frugally fashioned Bel Air and Biscayne. The taillight trim panel—also known as a cove panel—returned to the design plans one year later.

The thin roof pillars on the sports coupes were not identical but very similar to the 1960 models. The back window was huge and featured compound curves for a wraparound and wrap-over look that was commonly referred to as the "bubble top." The bubble tops had a space-age look, mimicking the canopy on fighter jets. Visibility was great, but the sun beating down on rear-seat passengers or on the upholstery exacted a toll.

Four-door hardtops were still in demand, and the Chevy was a handsome model. Its wider, more formally designed rear pillars were a sign of things to come. The design was applied to the sports coupes in 1962. This squared-off roofline proved to be a much-appreciated improvement for the comfort of rear-seat passengers because of increased headroom and protection from the sun.

As in 1960, the engine options consisted of a 235-ci six cylinder, a 283-ci V-8, and a 348-ci V-8. The basic Impala was equipped with a three-speed manual transmission and the 170-horsepower 283 engine. Optional transmissions included a four-speed manual, the two-speed automatic Powerglide, and the commercially unsuccessful three-speed automatic Turboglide. The four-speed manual and the Turboglide were not optional with six-cylinder engines, and the Turboglide was not available with engines producing more than 305 horsepower. The 348 engines and the Turboglide transmissions were phased out of production in 1961.

In the January 1961 *Motor Trend* magazine, two Impalas were compared: one with the 250-horsepower 348-ci engine and a Turboglide automatic transmission, and the other with the 170-horsepower 283. The magazine reported that "the performance of both engines was lively," with the

283 less than 2 seconds slower in a 0–60 miles per hour sprint. Times were reported as 10.3 seconds for the 348 and 12.2 for the 283. The bigger engine won accolades, however, when tested in the acceleration from 40 to 70 miles per hour, and was judged as "far superior" in passing speeds. *Motor Trend* also praised the more expensive Turboglide transmission for its "steady, but powerful, thrust with no perceptible shift points."

The Impala suspension, the same as on all Chevrolets, relied on coil springs and shock absorbers on all four corners. *Motor Trend*'s test drivers concluded the "somewhat softer than average" springing provided "a smooth ride at any speed," and credited its ability to absorb small road shocks as "probably the best in Chevrolet's class." Although nicked for considerable body lean when cornering, overall handling was considered excellent.

Once again the Impala proved to be a standout when it came to comfort and convenience for driver and passengers. The look and feel of luxury at a Chevy price was the Impala's hallmark. Materials such as carpeting, side panels, trim, and hardware put the Impala into a class with medium-priced luxury cars. The biggest improvement over the 1960 model was the ease of entry and exit. The much-cursed dog leg on the leading edge of the front doors was all but eliminated, the doors were wider, the seat benches were higher off the floorboards, and the transmission tunnel was less intrusive. Impalas continued to use a special sports-style steering wheel with "lightning holes" in the metal spokes.

The instrument panel was redesigned for the 1961 models. The three-pod style with a large circular speedometer in the center, which was a popular 1950's style, was replaced with an open-face design featuring a long horizontal speedometer. Overall the effect was more simplified and less glitzy. The steering wheel also gained a more sophisticated look that related to the Impala's quest for a more luxurious status. For driver convenience, the glovebox

On a sunny day, rear-seat passengers wouldn't get much shade in the sport coupe. Interior fabrics were subject to fading and cracking due to the extreme effects of the sun. *Zone Five Photo*

was relocated to the center of the instrument panel. Standard Impala features included an electric clock, a parking-brake warning light, backup lights, higher-quality carpeting, fingertip door releases, and custom-length armrests (with safety reflectors).

The Impala remained a highly optioned car. Among the most popular features to accessorize the new Impala were luxury items such as air conditioning, tinted glass, power steering, power brakes, power windows, and power seats. Impala could deliver a lot of luxury at a reasonable price most people could afford. Driving a Chevy was not particularly prestigious, but driving an Impala was.

Impala also was making a name as a performance car. The tri-powered 348 was a seriously powerful engine when equipped with 9.5:1 compression heads, dual exhaust, a high-lift cam, and mechanical lifters. This would be the fourth and final year for the 348 engines, which were introduced the same year as the Impala. Along with the 348 engine, the tri-power (three deuces) carburetor treatment was also retired. The responsibility of keeping the competition at bay in the future was put on the shoulders of the 409. Its success made the 348's passing barely noticeable.

The performance-minded buyer in 1961 looked down the order list and also found popular choices such as Posi-Traction (limited-slip rear end), a heavy-duty battery, plus heavy-duty brakes, springs, shocks, and clutch.

The popularity of these items prompted Chevrolet to introduce the first Super Sport package in the early summer of 1961. It was a defining moment in the history of Impala and the Chevrolet Division. The Super Sport badge was golden, and in the beginning it was solely an Impala option.

The 1961 Impala Super Sport option was technically available on any body style, but in subsequent years it would be limited to only sport coupes and convertibles. Production figures weren't tabulated on the individual models of Super Sports, but it is estimated that 450 were sold during the final months of the 1961 run. The only sales brochure for the 1961 Super Sport features a four-door hardtop, although none of these are known to have been built.

Here's what you got as part of the dress-up kit: special SS emblems on the quarter panels and deck lid; unique, tri-bar, spinner-type wheel covers; the passenger-side assist bar mounted on the dash; a padded instrument panel; and a Sun tachometer mounted on the steering column in the 10

Script *Impala* and the Impala emblem dress up the side trim, which is unique to the top-of-the-line nameplate. Impala badges would become more numerous on future models. *Zone Five Photo*

Inside, the 1961 Impala featured a new instrument console. Standard items in the Impala included electric clock, parking-brake warning light, backup lights, rich carpeting, fingertip door releases, and long armrests with built-in safety reflectors. This interior includes a tachometer and floor-mounted four-speed shifter. *Zone Five Photo*

o'clock position. But the most important option couldn't be found on any price list. It was the pride of ownership that this flagship Impala brought with it. Corvette had always been the image-building sports car in the Chevy lineup. But with the introduction of the Super Sport Impala, the Corvette had company. Chevrolet bred America's sports car with America's full-size favorite. The SS would lead Impala and Chevrolet on a march through the 1960s that would deliver unprecedented popularity and set Impala on a course to be the best-selling nameplate in history.

The SS package in 1961 was truly a performance package. Nothing less than the high-performance 348 engines or the new 409 could be ordered. The 348 options were 305-, 340-, or 350-horsepower engines and the 409 was rated at 360 horses. Transmission choices were the two-speed Powerglide automatic (305-horse 348 only) or the four-speed manual. The four-speed cars were equipped with a bright metal transmission cover plate at the base of the shifter. Other standard features on the 1961 SS models were power steering, power brakes, 8.00-14/4 ply narrow whitewall tires, and heavy-duty brakes, shocks, and springs. A 409-powered 1961 Super Sport Impala remains one of the most rare and desirable Impala collectibles.

Dial 409 for a Real Fine Time

Replacing the 348 engine as Chevy's big horse in mid-1961 was the 409. A quick look at the 409 and the sibling resemblance to the 348 is obvious. The most noticeable difference was the silver-painted valve covers. The factory-style covers on the 348 were orange. A common misconception is that the 409 and 348 engine castings were one and the same. The truth is that a beefier crankshaft in the 409 required changes to the bottom end. On closer examination, there's plenty of good stuff that distinguishes this engine from its 348 predecessor. Anyone who says it is a bored and stroked 348 is only about 10 percent right.

From the beginning the differences were substantial, and in quick fashion it was upgraded with performance enhancements that made it the king of the street and strip. Camshaft improvements were important factors as was the bigger, better four-barrel carburetor that lurked under the air cleaner. During the 409's evolution, new heads, featuring larger ports and valves, and increasingly progressive camshaft grinds that provided higher lift were introduced. Separate manifolds were designed for the single four-barrel carb setup and for the dual quad carburetors. Redesigned pistons were also added, which accommodated higher compression.

At its coming-out party the 409 was rated at 360 horsepower. With the noted improvements, horsepower ratings rose to 380 with the single Carter carb and 409 with the twin Carter four-barrel carbs. From the get go, these engines took advantage of solid lifters and 11:25:1 compression.

Motor Trend test drives of the 409-powered SS—wearing stock tires and with factory exhaust— resulted in 14.02-second quarter-mile times (98.14 miles per hour). These were heady accomplishments for a full-size car, aided somewhat by using the ultra-low 4.56 rear-end gears.

CHAPTER 4

Can It Get Any Better than This?

"The very essence of leadership is that you have to have a vision."

—*Theodore Hesburgh*

When the 1962 Impalas hit the showrooms, the momentum of the Super Sport option package was beginning to reverberate through the cities, towns, and countryside of America. In anticipation of big things to come, Chevrolet added some design touches to the appearance package and dropped the performance engine requirement. The introduction of the 327-ci V-8, a Chevrolet star for many years to come, coincided nicely with the broadening of the SS engine options. It came as no surprise to anyone that the popularity of the Impala SS surged. In the coming years the SS would be like gasoline on fire. It was red hot.

It was a good year for automobile sales and the U.S. economy in general. Many businesses realized record or

The new roofline for the 1962 sport coupe had a crisp, clean line that approximated a taut convertible top. The inset area on the full-length body side molding was painted a contrasting color that added highlight to the car. Perfect examples are a red inset on a black car and a silver inset on a red car. *Late Great Chevy Collection*

The thin-pillar design that was popular from 1959 through 1961 was retired from the Impala line in favor of a more formal roofline in 1962. Although the sport coupes and convertibles garnered most of the attention, the four-door sedan was also a handsome automobile. *1978–1999 GM Corp. Used with permission of GM Media Archives*

near-record gains. Auto sales spiked to levels that had not been attained since the record-breaking year of 1955. Once again Chevrolet introduced a new model for the entry-level buyer. To run alongside the rear-engine, rear-drive Corvair was the new-for-1962 Chevy II. Its base-level approach to transportation needs didn't make a dent in Impala sales, but it clearly was an option to the full-size Biscayne. More importantly it was another indicator of General Motors' plan toward niche market fulfillment. The same approach was under way at Ford as Falcons, Fairlanes, and Thunderbirds competed with the full-size Galaxie. This segmented market approach was just a few years beyond the one-Ford-for-everyone proposition that existed previously.

Redesigning the Impala for 1962 was a matter of cleaning up the items on the 1961 model that tied it to the 1950s-era cars. Because the Impala vision in most minds was the sport coupe body style, it is appropriate to focus attention on that. One of the more obvious ties to the old decade was the hardtop roofline that made use of extremely thin pillars. Along with this, the windshield and the rear window glass wrapped upward into the roof, creating a significant glass area. The 1962 sport coupe design successfully implemented a formal roofline with the appearance of a crisply creased convertible top. The artful execution of that roofline design was a significant contribution to the ongoing success of the Impala sport coupe and therefore the entire Impala lineup. It was an Impala exclusive in 1962.

The Bel Air sport coupe continued with the "bubble top" for another year. Many Chevy enthusiasts love the bubble tops, but at the time it was a connection to the past and Impala was looking toward the future. It also gave Impala the opportunity to have an exclusive sport coupe to go along with the only full-size convertible in the Chevy lineup. The two-door sedan (or post coupe) was also

dropped from the Impala inventory. It too was relegated to Bel Air status. The four-door sport sedan (four-door hardtop), the traditional four-door sedan, and a station wagon were also Impala options. In the case of the station wagon, it was the first year the Impala nameplate was attached.

Although clearly a face-lift redesign, the 1962 Impala made significant improvements. Looking head-on at the Impala, the hood was flatter and the grille gained a more powerful appearance, due in large part to the egg-crate pattern and an angular top edge/leading edge design. In comparison the 1961 looks rather blunt and square. The headlights were placed within aluminum bezels and were somewhat recessed into the grille, providing a slightly sinister appearance. A thicker front bumper added mass to a front-end design that had been implementing a thinner, lighter appearance since 1959.

The spear-like side molding was simplified and moved to the top of the fender line, passing over the top of the door handles on its route from the top of the headlights to the top of the rear panel fascia. It was more slender than the 1961 version, and the stainless-steel trim outlined a painted area that color-matched the interior. On the Super Sport trim, the center area was filled with a swirled engine-turned aluminum panel rather than the painted insert. A full-length crease in the sheet metal from headlight to taillight—passing just above the wheelwheels and well under the door handles—provided a second visual clue that the Impala was long and lean.

Bright ornamental windsplits, perched upon the front fenders, were standard Impala embellishments. These doo-dads are often associated with cars of the late 1950s, but they remained popular markers for status cars well into the 1960s. The simulated exhaust ports below the rear window on the Impala hardtops were another example of styling

The redesign of the squared-off 1961 Impala led to a more rakish style in 1962. The top of the grille leans forward into the wind, and the slope of the rear deck provides a more aerodynamic appearance. *1978–1999 GM Corp. Used with permission of GM Media Archives*

Rounded taillights (three for Impalas, two for lesser models) carried over from the previous year, but the rearend styling was cleaner and simpler. The aluminum taillight panel and the fluted rocker moldings were both part of the Impala trim package. *1978-1999 GM Corp. Used with permission of GM Media Archives.*

expression that tended to be overused on the 1950s-era cars. Attention to small details such as these, and to items such as wheel cover design, added an undeniable sex appeal.

Another Impala-only feature was the sill trim that protected the lower portion of the body between the front and rear wheels. This feature was used on the original 1958 Impala, but had been absent from the standard features since. Without this protection, the paint in this area picked up numerous stone chips and quickly looked tattered. For this same reason, the aluminum trim pieces also took a beating. Beyond the issue of functionality, the brightwork added a touch of class. It tends to look better on cars with side trim placed closer to the beltline and with less overall brightwork, which is part of the reason it works better on the 1962 Impala than it did on the 1958.

The Impala Super Sport models attract the greatest attention at car shows today, and they were admired just as intensely in 1962. Rather than offering the SS package of sporty trim options on every body style, Chevy limited production to only the sport coupes and convertibles. And rather than limiting engine choices to only the high-performance mills, every Chevy engine became an option. Chevrolet rightly figured that more buyers would like the SS looks without the necessity of buying high-performance equipment, so the heavy-duty suspension parts were no longer part of the package either.

The biggest change from 1961 was that front bucket seats with a short console in between became part of the package in 1962. The vinyl upholstery, additional bright trim inside and out, and the Super Sport badges provided

the style points. It was up to the buyer to decide whether the engine and transmission could back up the swagger. In 1961 fewer than 500 Impalas received the Super Sport treatment. By the end of the 1962 model run, nearly 100,000 Impala buyers wanted SS initials on their cars.

There continued to be a long list of accessories that could be added to both the Impala and Impala SS. Those that addressed luxury and convenience included air conditioning in standard and deluxe versions, power brakes, power steering, power windows, power seats, outside and inside rearview mirrors, two-speed electric wipers with washers, tinted windows, and manual or push-button radios. Accessories for the performance enthusiast included the Posi-Traction rear axle, heavy-duty items such as brakes, clutch, radiator, battery, springs and shocks, plus dual exhaust and temperature-controlled radiator fan.

1962 Impala Super Sport Equipment List

Bucket-type front seats with console
Passenger assist bar
Special emblems, wheel covers, side molding insert, rear cove molding (engine-turned style)
Bright-metal transmission cover plate for four-speed

Like a loyal hunting dog, you could count on the 283-ci engine to be at your call with the 1962 Impala. It was as faithful and true as any engine could be, and since its inception in 1957 it brought satisfaction to more motorists than any other engine in America. Previously available with a four-barrel, high-compression option, in 1962 Chevy saw fit to only offer it in its economical two-barrel, 170-horsepower configuration. That wasn't a surprise. It was this tamer version that was by far the most popular. An additional reason was that the new 327-ci engine was slotted to become the high-performance small block. The 327 took the 283 block and built horsepower the old-fashioned way by increasing bore and stroke. In the past the performance-oriented 283s pumped up the muscle with fuel injection

Engine Options

Cylinders	cid	Carburetors	Horsepower
Inline 6	235	single-barrel	135
V-8	283	two barrel	170
V-8	327	four barrel	250
V-8	327	four barrel	300
V-8	409	four barrel	380*
V-8	409	dual four barrel	409**

* includes high-lift cam, dual exhaust, 8.00-14/4-ply blackwall tires, and heavy-duty springs and shocks

**includes high-lift cam, mechanical lifters, dual exhaust, 8.00-14/4 ply blackwall tires, and heavy-duty springs and shocks - Turbo Fire 409

(1957–1959). These engines could really wail, but in terms of day in and day out dependability, even a TV weatherman was a better bet. The 327 made use of high compression (10.5 to 1), a four-barrel carb, and a wilder cam to deliver 250 horsepower—the same as the base 348 of one year earlier. Choosing the bigger Carter carb and its special manifold and cylinder heads kicked in an extra 50 horsepower. Both engines were fitted with dual exhausts. The 327s could be matched up with a three- or four-speed manual transmission or with the Powerglide. The variable-pitch

Turboglide quietly slipped into oblivion at the end of the 1961 model year.

The Chevy performance fanatics were still buzzing about the limited introduction of the big-block 409 at the halfway point of the 1961 model year. Refinements were made to the head, piston design, main bearings, and intake valves. The single four-barrel carburetor was larger than the year before, but the big banana was a dual four-barrel carb setup. The advertised 409 horsepower was widely accepted as being well shy of the true potential.

The brushed aluminum cove panel surrounding the taillights once again provided a distinctive Impala trademark. A similar panel on the 1960 Impala was broken in two by the license plate. Here the license plate was relocated below the bumper, allowing for an uninterrupted, and more beautiful, rear-end design. *Zone Five Photo*

A panorama of paint choices continued to be offered. In a single color there was black, gold, two reds, two greens, four blues, silver, black, white, cream, beige, and a special Anniversary Gold—used on sport coupes only. The anniversary was Chevrolet Division's 50th, and gold Chevrolet trademarks were used in the hood and deck emblems of the 1962 Impalas and other Chevys. Two-toning was still popular, with 10 options to choose from. Interiors were available in seven separate colors, and even convertible tops could be ordered with a choice of four different colors.

Chevy by the Numbers in 1962

Total Chevy sales reached nearly 1,600,000
Full-size Chevy sales exceeded 1,000,000
Impala sales exceeded 700,000

1963 Impala: Big and Bold and Beautiful

During the five years since the Impala debuted, Chevrolet continued to pile up record years for sales and production. It wasn't a soaring uninterrupted climb with sales records set each year along the way, but it was unquestionably a streak that kept Ford looking up the ladder hoping Chevrolet would miss a step or slip a rung. It never happened. Led by the high-flying Impala, the division relentlessly raised the bar in the low-price field by adding comfort, convenience, and performance options to the Chevrolet name. Car buyers responded to the idea of a Chevrolet built in the image of Cadillac by beating a path to the Chevy dealerships. The full-size Chevrolet was still in the driver seat, but the forces of change were building momentum. Corvair and Chevy II were well on their way to establishing a new entry-level point for the Chevy buyer. That buyer used to start shopping for Chevrolets with Biscayne or Bel Air and work up to Impala. Not only that, but Chevy was getting ready to introduce yet another inexpensive car to fill in the gap between compact and full-size cars.

Plymouth, with its introduction of new models in 1962, made the decision to downsize its full-size cars. Rather than take on the expense of a separate line of intermediate-size cars, Plymouth's Fury, Belvedere, and Savoy were scaled back to fit the newly developing market. The plan failed miserably. Either the downsizing strategy was flawed because buyers weren't willing to accept less from brand names that were built on providing more, or it simply didn't have a chance given the meat-loaf designs the company was trying to sell as steak. The result just about choked Plymouth to death. It took them years to get back on track with a strategy that once again put Plymouth in its traditional role of building full-size, midsize, and compact competitors to Ford and Chevrolet.

Conversely, Impala was the right product at the right time. And the brand name was golden. It delivered exceptional value in a package that offered quality as well as performance, style, size and comfort, and the reputation of leadership. Ford's full-size flagship, the Galaxie, was also an extremely popular car during this era. Nonetheless, the

Slide in behind the wheel of a 1962 Impala convertible. Top-down driving could vary from mild to wild depending on the owner's choice of engines: 409, 327, 283, and 235. *Zone Five Photo*

The only Chevrolet specifically produced for drag racing was the 1963 Impala limited-edition model known as the Z-11. Factory records indicate there were 57 Impalas built with the special speed equipment: a racing-prepared 427-ci engine, plus aluminum fenders, bumpers, and hood. *James J. Genat*

More people chose Chevrolet's four-door sedan than any other body style in 1963. With few exceptions, this car was America's favorite car year in and year out throughout the 1960s. It was undeniably handsome, as dependable as the day was long, and most importantly, it was recognized as sensible transportation. *1978–1999 GM Corp. Used with permission of GM Media Archives*

The Impala redesign in 1963 consisted of mostly minor face-lifting. Viewed from the front, it looked bigger and bolder than the 1962. The broad, flat hood used two slight windsplits rather than a single split down the center of the hood. *Zone Five Photo*

Impala was outselling it at nearly a two-to-one clip.

On many occasions and in many ways, cars get unfairly characterized as "merely face-lifts" of the previous model. Sometimes change is for the better and other times it is best to leave well enough alone. The Impala seemed to prosper regardless of whether design changes were major or minor, and seemingly without repercussions from the automobiles produced by its direct and indirect competitors. If Chevrolet's annual sales dipped, they did not fall as far as the auto industry in general. And in years when the industry-wide sales were up, Chevrolet sales were usually way up. Credit the Chevrolet design team for this unprecedented and uninterrupted run of success. The 1963 Impala production estimates exceeded 832,000.

The 1963 Impala was one of those successful face-lift designs. Remember that automobile designs are approved at least three years before they roll off assembly lines and long before public opinion produces sales that dictate success or failure. The sales success of the 1962 Impala indicates the design was right on the money. Even with the current advantage of comparing it to cars that came before and after the 1962, it's difficult to fault it. To its credit the 1963 was different enough to create a distinction and a positive impression, but not so much as to bastardize the excellent original design.

Impala was enjoying the fruits of a tremendous reputation. Its all-American image was right up there with hot dogs and apple pie, and years down the road Chevy advertising would remind us of just that fact. In today's marketing-driven world, it's called brand image. In 1963, Chevy had all the brand image it could possibly want or need.

Comparing the 1963 with the 1962, the Chevy family resemblance is apparent in features such as the trademark taillights, the egg-crate–style grille, and the full body-length side trim and sheet-metal crease. Chevrolet introduced seven new paint colors to further the distinction between new and old models. That brought the total number of paint-color options to 26: 15 single colors and 11 two-tone options.

The Impala image was bolstered in 1963 when the immensely popular two-door sport coupe body style once again became an Impala exclusive. A vinyl roof was introduced as an option on the 1963 Impala sport coupe only. It could be ordered in either black or white. Sport coupe sales nearly reached 200,000 units in 1963. And the four-door sports sedan, which was also an Impala-only body style, was close behind. Together they were great for the Impala image as really cool wheels for young adults. Meanwhile, the Bel Air series—which as recently as 1957 was the focus of Chevy attention—was left with the more mundane two-door and four-door sedans. That was bad for

Inside, the Impala featured considerable room and an expansive instrument panel. The vents above the radio identify this car as an air conditioned model, and the engine-turned aluminum trim was a Super Sport trademark. *Zone Five Photo*

Super Sport was more of an appearance package than a performance package, but often it was the best of both worlds. The 409 was the engine of choice for the performance-minded drivers. It was tightly packed into the engine compartment, and was one of the most powerful street performers of its day. *Zone Five Photo*

the Bel Air image, but not the bottom line. Sedans, particularly four-door sedans, handily outsold all other body styles. In the Impala series, the four-door sedans outsold the sport coupes by just about a two-to-one ratio.

Another step away from the 1950s was the demise of the wraparound windshield, which was with Chevrolet since 1955. Without the wraparound windshield, straight windshield pillars replaced the bowed style that had been the norm since 1959. The trend toward wider, flatter hoods continued, and the single windsplit down the mid-

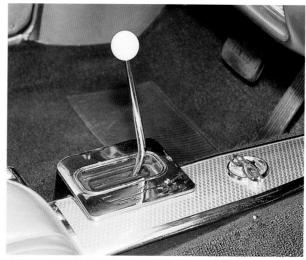

A floor-mounted shifter (in this case with the cue-ball shifter knob and mated with an automatic transmission), bucket seats, and a console were all a part of the SS package. All-vinyl upholstery replaced fabric in the SS package. *Zone Five Photo*

dle was replaced by twin windsplits aimed at the driver and front-seat passenger.

The taillight cove area was once again surrounded with a brushed aluminum trim piece as part of the Impala-only package. Other Impala-only features included two short, bright-metal stripes attached to the leading edge of the front fenders. Impala watchers would remember a similar treatment used back in 1960. And the narrow side-trim spear with a painted inset was prominent once again, but for 1963 it split the side view of the car through the middle. Super Sport models once again made effective use of the fancy engine-turned aluminum within the side spear and the taillight cove area. Body panels below the beltline were all new.

Overall the design was slightly more luxurious, and the cars appeared heavier due in large part to the grille design, which provided a more massive appearance when viewed from the perspective of oncoming traffic. The bumper design also added to this big-car likeness. More "substantial" might be a friendlier way to describe it. Chevrolet referred to it as "big and bold." Not since the 1958 Impala had there been such an overt effort to be more like Cadillac in appearance. And with its soft coil-spring suspension, Impala enjoyed a "big car" smooth ride that was welcomed by the traditional buyers of low-cost transportation.

Inside, the Impala also excelled. The layout and design and the quality of materials combined to create an almost ideal environment. The SS option sizzled with sex appeal. Soft, vinyl-covered bucket seats, a shiny full-length console, a sport-style steering wheel, and plenty of SS identification all

A red 1963 Impala convertible with a 409 under the hood was the automotive equivalent of Mickey Mantle or Elizabeth Taylor. People would stop and stare. They still do. *Zone Five Photo*

You've a lot to look for under our sign

More than just an ordinary used car lot.
For one thing, you'll find an extraordinary
selection of used Chevies and other makes.
From convertibles to pickup trucks. All with
plenty of unused miles.
For another, you'll meet an experienced
salesman who's also a used car specialist. When
you ask questions, he'll give you straight
answers—the kind of answers that will help

you make a good choice when you buy.
And, just as if you'd bought a new car, your
Chevy dealer's highly trained service staff is
there to help you if you ever need it.
So, when you're thinking of buying a good
used car or a serviceable truck, remember
your Chevrolet dealer's OK sign. It stands for
a lot.... Chevrolet Division of General Motors,
Detroit, Michigan.

Just another used car? Maybe in 1964 or 1965, but a 1963 Impala convertible would be more than just OK today. Funny thing is you can still buy one for less than the cost of the average new car.

reinforced the attention to details that evoked owner pride and increased customer satisfaction levels. Much of the success of the standard Impala was attributable to that same attention to details. Impala color schemes and fabrics provided more choices than Howard Johnson had flavors of ice cream. It was as nice as many of the more expensive cars with its rich-looking carpets and vinyl upholstery. The instrument panel was impressive, too, despite the use of idiot lights rather than true gauges. The fuel indicator was the only real gauge. To reduce the amount of glare, the instruments were more deeply recessed within a wide, horizontal cluster. Overall the Impala was big and comfortable (in a purely 1960s way), with room enough for six travelers and everyone's luggage.

The Super Sport Impala was Chevrolet's pin-up girl. And their advertising flashed that image with great success. From every angle this car had great allure, and it willingly purred "Take me home." The seduction worked. The Impala Super Sport popularity swelled. According to production estimates, more than 150,000 Super Sport coupes and convertibles were built in 1963. The Super Sport extras were essentially the same as in 1962, but the presentation reflected minor styling changes to the SS emblems, the SS wheel covers, and the trim pieces. The use of engine-turned aluminum for much of the interior and exterior highlights continued to enjoy widespread appeal.

To provide more options in the range of horsepower, Chevrolet introduced a 340-horsepower version of the big-block 409. With a lower compression, hydraulic lifters, and a milder cam, this engine was much more conducive to everyday driving than the two rowdy racing versions that were upgraded from 380 to 400 and 409 to 425 horsepower. The 409s came with chrome valve covers, chrome air cleaner housing, and a 6,000-rpm tachometer mounted on the dash.

The two 327 options were once again rated at 250 and 300 horsepower, and the 283, by virtue of new heads and an improved cam, was pumped up to 195 horsepower. It was far and away the most popular of the engine options with more than three-quarters of a million slipped into 1963 Chevys.

Not an Impala favorite, but available nonetheless, was the 140-horse inline six. This six-cylinder engine was a much-improved seven-main-bearing design, a vast improvement over the previous six that had evolved from the old "Stove Bolt" six dating back to the late 1920s. Another notable change that affected all Chevy engines was the use of alternators over generators.

Impala interior design was an artful blend of information and entertainment. Controls were within easy reach and simple to use. Most enthusiasts wanted real gauges instead of "idiot lights" for oil, temperature, and amps, but other than that, there were no complaints. The overall look and feel of the materials gave buyers more than their money's worth. *Zone Five Photo*

If you build it, they will come. The slogan worked for a ball field in an Iowa cornfield and for the Chevrolet Impala—the most popular car in mid-1960s America. Chevy factories hummed with activity. Americans hummed "See the USA in your Chevrolet." *1978–1999 GM Corp. Used with permission of GM Media Archives*

The full-length side trim moved up and down from year to year. In 1963 it was at bumper height. In 1962 it passed above the door handle, and in 1961 it was midway between the 1962 and 1963 locations. That seemingly small styling element played an important role in determining whether the car looked lighter and faster, or heavier and more luxurious. *Zone Five Photo*

Previous Page
The traditional Chevy egg-crate–style grille was better some years than others. This is one of the best. An optional grille guard with rubber bullets on each end dresses up this Impala and protects the aluminum grille from the parking lot demolition derby drivers. *Zone Five Photo*

The 1964 Impala, shown here as an Impala SS, was even more popular than the 1963. Although the redesign was relatively minor, the car gained a more luxurious stature with both the front and rear squared off. The result was a more formal appearance. For the first time the Impala SS became a separate model rather than an option package. *1978–1999 GM Corp. Used with permission of GM Media Archives*

As was the case in 1962, fender emblems and numerals indicated which engine was under the hood.

Transmission options included the Powerglide automatic, plus three- and four-speed manuals. The Powerglide was not available with the 400- and 425-horsepower engines, and the four speeds were not an option on the 230- and 283-ci engines. Overdrive was offered on both the six and the small V-8, however. In keeping with the policy of providing customers with plenty of options, rear axle ratios ranged from a high of 3.08 to a low of 4.56. In between were 3.36, 3.55, 3.70 (overdrive only), and 4.11. The ultra-low 4.56 and the 4.11s were only matched up with the 400- and 425-horsepower engines.

1964 Impala: The Hits Just Keep Coming

Chevrolet had something new and enticing to offer when the 1964 models debuted. Surprisingly it was not the face-lifted-once-again Impala. Why not? No other model had ever dominated the market like Impala. On one front it was rewarding Chevrolet by becoming America's blue-collar Cadillac. On another, in its Super Sport trim, it was the most popular full-size performance car available. Yet it was the introduction of a new intermediate-size Chevrolet, the Chevelle, that created a buzz.

Not only was this the third new line of cars Chevy had introduced since 1960, it was the first one capable of hav-

On the Super Sport models the designers placed the side trim in the headlight-to-taillight position, which somewhat counteracted the overall heavy appearance. From a distance, it's a quick way to differentiate an SS from an Impala. *Zone Five Photo*

Wider bumpers gave the Impala the appearance of a bigger, heavier, more expensive car. Parking lights were incorporated into the bumpers, which helped break up the wall of chrome and aluminum. The egg-crate grille design remained an important element. *Zone Five Photo*

ing an effect on the Impala. Although not an immediate threat to the Impala regime, within a few years the Chevelle, particularly the Super Sport models, would be stealing the Impala's thunder as well as its customers.

With the Chevelle, the Chevy II, and the Corvair combining to provide low-cost, entry-level Chevrolets for customers wanting compact and midsize cars, there was no reason to look back when designing ever-bigger Impalas. The fact that Cadillac flavor remained a major influence on the Impala could be seen in the formal styling and more elegant interiors.

The face-lifted 1964 Impala shared the same basic structural members, rooflines, glass area, and doors with the 1963. Front and rear redesigns gave Chevrolets a more blunt appearance. In side view, the sheet metal was sculpted with the lower recess lining up with the upper edge of the bumpers and the higher recess matching up with the tops of the taillights and the center point in the headlights. The recess was outlined with an anodized aluminum trim piece on the standard Impala. The Super Sport side trim was a single spear placed just above the recess.

The cove area surrounding the taillights lost the full anodized aluminum trim panel that brought distinction to the 1962 and 1963 Impalas. The trademark six round tail-

Badges were always an important element on the Super Sport Impalas, or any of the other Chevy SS models. They could be found on rear quarter panels and the right rear portion of the trunk lid in 1964. *Zone Five Photo*

Convertible production was off ever so slightly from the 1963 peak, but that still resulted in nearly 82,000 automobiles. Impala production overall continued to increase; the total for the 1964 model year was only a few hundred short of 890,000. *Zone Five Photo*

Once again the 409 was king of the hill. Factory-announced horsepower ratings were 340, 400, and 425, depending on the buyer's selection of carbs, cams, and compression. *Zone Five Photo*

lights were more elegantly styled with bright trim rings to set them off. A horizontal trim bar on the rear edge of the deck lid with corners that curved downward around the outboard taillight to meet the rear bumper highlighted the rear design. Redesigned bumpers were another visual clue that Chevrolet was pursuing a more Cadillac-like image. They were thicker, and created a visual effect that made the car appear lower and heavier.

The inclination to formalize the overall appearance of the Chevrolet was also apparent in the restyled grille. For the last two years Chevrolet had utilized an angular grille with a leading edge that was suggestive of speed. The 1964 grille was flat and vertical, somewhat similar to the wall-like facade that was used in 1958 to effectively connect that Impala to the Cadillac image of luxury.

That's not to say the 1964 Impala did not have a

sport/performance image. As was always the case, in Super Sport trim a perfectly handsome Impala became more fiercely fit, like a heavyweight champion in his prime. The formula for this success was pretty much the same as it had been for the previous SS models: tri-bar wheel covers, the engine-turned swirl pattern on the side moldings, rear cove molding, instrument panel and console, and the strategic placement of the SS badges. For the first time, Chevrolet kept track of the Super Sport Impalas as a separate series rather than as an Impala option package.

Building on its past success, Super Sport production jumped from 150,000 to more than 185,000. Right alongside was a bump in Impala sales from 832,000 to nearly 890,000. Comparisons of Chevy's Impala and Bel Air show the Impala outproducing the Bel Air by well over 550,000 cars, and that's without factoring in the Super Sports. Top-of-the-line models are not supposed to outsell their lower-priced

Impala sport coupes had size and swagger. The hardtop roofline had a crisp, buttoned-down look that had been consistent since 1962. In 1964 the sport coupe body style was once again exclusive to Impala (Bel Air was cut out of the action). Incredibly, the production more than doubled. The total topped 442,000. *Zone Five Photo*

Side trim on the Impala differed from the Super Sport. Rather than the single spear, a dual molding was implemented. It followed the body contour from headlight to taillights, then made a reverse C and passed just over the rear wheelwell and forward to the front wheelwell. *1978–1999 GM Corp. Used with permission of GM Media Archives*

siblings. That's an indicator of how hot Impala had become.

Another key statistic was the dramatic demand for sport coupes, which were only available as an Impala or an Impala SS. In 1963 this model showed potential by hitting the 200,000 level, but in 1964 sales topped 442,000. Those kinds of numbers were encroaching on the normally untouchable production figures for four-door sedans, which included Impala, Bel Air, and Biscayne. Combining those three lines, Chevy sold 536,000 four-door sedans in 1964. Sport coupes are not supposed to rival four-door sedans for production supremacy. Impala's achievement was almost unbelievable.

The usual Impala upgrades were still in place—basically, greater attention to details in the overall design and in the little things like trim and fabrics and paint. Among the standard details that set the Impala apart from the lower echelon of full-size Chevys was the chrome-capped single windsplit down the center of the wide, flat hood. The same treatment on the deck lid was anodized aluminum. And as

before, the Impalas were dressed up with stainless-steel reveal and windshield moldings. Inside there were bright-metal moldings around the windshield, rear window, and the roof rails. An Impala-only steering wheel, an electric clock, and an emergency-brake warning light were among the benefits. One by one the items don't seem like much, but together they put Impala in a league of its own.

Die-hard drag racers were miffed that Chevrolet wasn't pushing the horsepower and torque ratings through the roof, causing the 409 to drop a rung or two on the power charts. But the big, if somewhat old, mill was still garnering a fair share of respect on the street. And the other engine options were solid performers with a better mix of performance and reliability than any other manufacturer could offer. Across the board, the engine displacements remained the same as 1963: 230-ci six, and 283-, 327-, and 409-ci V-8s.

Why mess with success? People loved the Impala. They loved the looks, the engines, the ride, and the reliability. No need to change for the sake of change.

Looking at the suspension, however, it was evident that sometimes change was needed. The suspension was the one major element that still tied these Impalas to the original 1958 edition. Very little had changed over seven model years. Not an exceptionally long run for a chassis (actually quite average), but if any area of the Impala cried out for updating, this was it. The X-member frame with four cross-members and box girder side rails was ready for retirement. And the same could be said for the independent suspension featuring coil springs with concentric shock absorbers.

They say, "If it ain't broke, don't fix it." But that's only good advice in the short term. Chevy was planning ahead to avoid a "broken" Impala. And there would be changes.

Drop-top Impala Production

Year	Totals
1961	56,742
1962	68,442
1963	82,659
1964	81,897

CHAPTER 5

Records Are Meant to be Broken

"Don't be afraid to take a big step. You can't cross a chasm in two small jumps."

—*David Lloyd George*

From day one, the Chevrolet mission was to design and build the Impala to prove luxury and performance could be presented in an affordable package. Or, at the very least, it was created so people who saw themselves as "Chevy folks" could enjoy the special stuff previously reserved for the owners of more expensive brands. And, of course, it was critically important that a Chevy provided more for the money than a Ford or a Plymouth. Chevy made that part look easy in the decade from 1955 to 1965, providing indisputable sales results for the entire division, and establishing the Chevy reputation with a completely new group of young buyers. The Impala was the crowning achievement. For tens of millions of people, an Impala was something special.

Value was crucial, and the Impala was packed with value. A big part of that value was delivered by the design team, which was led by the boisterous Bill Mitchell. The

Grille design for both the 1965 and 1966 Impalas put more emphasis on the horizontal bars, which added to the wide-track look. A sliver of trim on the rocker panel provided a better-defined outline of the car. *Zone Five Photo*

The completely redesigned 1965 Chevy was highlighted by a sleek sport coupe that put the emphasis on sport and performance rather than formal luxury. The full-length side trim was eliminated, and it gave this Impala a clean, uninterrupted appearance. *1978–1999 GM Corp. Used with permission of GM Media Archives*

design fate of every General Motors vehicle came under Mitchell's scrutiny, and like his predecessor, Harley Earl, Mitchell dictated his vision with regard to car design. That's not to say he bent individual creative talents to his wishes. He had the best talent in the industry and he used it very effectively. However, GM automotive design in this era reflected his unmistakable influence and considerable talent.

The 1965 Chevy redesign was a monumental success story. Sales records that were set in 1955 were obliterated. At the conclusion of the 1965 model year nearly 2.4 million cars were sold. What was even more astounding was that almost 50 percent were wearing the Impala badge. Never in all of automotive history would a single nameplate sell that many cars in one model year. With the continued segmentation of the automotive market, it's unlikely that any other nameplate will soar higher than Impala. Thirty-five years have passed and the acclaim remains Impala property.

In terms of collectibility, the 1965 remains in the shadows, but quite possibly on the verge of a breakthrough. It is one of the best values in the collector car market. The design is clean and crisp, its overall appearance is athletically handsome, and the proportions are dead-on perfect. Performance packages include the last of the legendary 409s and the first of the renown 396s. Impala Super Sport convertibles and hardtops from 1965 could eventually be the most valuable of the highly collectible Impalas.

When these cars were first taking shape, the premise that longer and lower equaled better was still a basic doctrine. Although the 119-inch wheelbase was identical to the 1964 model's, the new Impala grew in overall length and increased its sleekness by dropping the roofline.

Every great automotive design has to have which hook that really affects people, makes them want to take a second look, a longer look. For the 1965 Impala it was that slippery sport coupe roofline that grabbed the most attention. The formal rooflines, popular from 1962 to 1964 on the sport coupes and sport sedans, were handsome and immensely popular. But after three years, there are good reasons to push on. Automotive design is almost always in motion, unless you want the Model T Ford or the Volkswagen Beetle. Chevrolet boldly made the change from 1964 to 1965. Bold moves can work well, or they can bite you in the behind. With this one swing, Chevy hit it out of the park. The result was a car, a Chevy, that looked fast even when it was sitting still. Not since the thin-pillared hardtop coupes of 1959–1961 had the Impala looked as streamlined.

The flowing roofline was beautifully integrated into the deck lid and rear quarter panels, and once again the six round Impala taillights stood out as distinctive and beautiful in their simplicity. Below the taillights and deck lid opening, but above the bumper, was a distinctive Impala trim panel that provided a finished look to the car's rear view. The brushed aluminum panel was silver-colored on Impalas and blacked out on the Super Sports. The Impala or Impala SS badge was positioned on this panel under the passenger-side taillight area.

An important element of the redesign was the higher beltline accentuated by the "Coke-bottle" bulge in the rear quarter panels, which added to the roundness that easily differentiated the car from the 1961–1964 series.

The return of the blade-type front bumper was an important aspect of designing this car to be less ponderous than the previous Impala. Bright moldings were used around the wheelwells on both the Impala and the Impala SS. The Impala also received trim on the rocker panels and lower edges of the rear quarter panels. *Late Great Chevy Collection*

The 1966 Impala was a mild face-lift of the all-new 1965. Front and rear sheet-metal changes resulted in a slightly more formal appearance. Impala sales remained strong, but couldn't match the records set in 1965. *1978–1999 GM Corp. Used with permission of GM Media Archives*

In sales literature Chevy referred to the "exciting new look of elegance," but this new look had a lot of sportiness to it. There was no argument—it had the look of a winner. It was fresh and new.

One notable change from Chevy tradition was the absence of side molding. And compared to 1964 models, the redesign made use of a lighter-looking, blade-style bumper treatment, which added to the Impala's sporty appearance that resonated agility and quickness. That played particularly well to those who preferred Impala to be a sport-oriented car and those who favored the sport coupes, sport sedans, and convertibles. Yet all this emphasis was accomplished with a vehicle with full-size car dimensions.

The blade-type front bumper was reminiscent of the design that was used effectively in 1959–1960. Those cars were also much lighter looking than the 1958 that preceded them. The front bumper and grille in 1965 were also styled with a mild V-shape, with the point of the V facing forward. This shape was accentuated by the windsplit down the center of the hood, and a crisp crease that split the bowtie emblem garnishing the sheet metal ahead of the hood.

The new design included frameless, curved, side glass that accentuated the aero-looking body contours, which included a bulging quarter panel over the rear wheels.

The grille design made use of dominant horizontal bars, adding to the perception that the new Impala was even wider than it was. The front bumper split the grille, with about one-third below the bumper. Quad headlights, each with an eyebrow of aluminum trim, were backed by an assembly that mimicked the grille design and added to the appearance of an ultra-wide grille. Amber turn signals were located beneath the bumper.

The long side-trim spears that Chevy for years had used to accentuate the length of their cars were abandoned on the 1965 Impala. There remained a strong character line, a crease in the sheet metal that was easily visible as it ran from headlights to taillights. But the absence of chrome decoration was a refreshing change. Brightwork highlighted the wheel openings, the rocker panels, and the lower extremes of the rear quarter panel. The Bel Air maintained the side spear tradition with a slender piece of brightwork.

Inside the Impala a new instrument panel design featured the long horizontal speedometer as its most prominent feature. A circular cluster of warning lights to the left of the speedometer was balanced on the end of the instrument panel with a circular clock face. The lower portion of the panel housed the controls for lights, wipers, ignition, lighter, and temperature controls. It was "dressed up" with

a dark-colored simulated wood-grain decal that was intended to remind owners of the luxurious appointments of more expensive cars. This panel was textured bright metal on the Super Sport Impalas. A long, thin Impala nameplate was placed across the glovebox door.

As was customary, the Impalas were nicely appointed with items such as the distinctive steering wheel, extra long armrests with the paddle-type door handles, deep-twist carpeting, and the ever popular rear-seat speaker grille that graced Impalas since 1958. Vent windows (ventipanes) were conveniently hand-crank operated rather than the cheaper clasp style used on lower-priced Chevelles, and the vinyl door panels were designed with a tufted appearance from the window frame down to a horizontal bright-metal trim piece below the armrests. Below the trim strip was a

Compared to the boxy style of the 1964, the 1965s and 1966s had curved body contours and a noticeable kickup on the tops of the rear quarter panels. Side glass was also curved. *Zone Five Photo*

textured scuff area. The choice of interior colors was extensive, a customer-oriented option from the days of the full-service gas station. The 1965 Impalas had seven interior color options. Textured fabrics were the most popular, but the cool look was the special all-vinyl black interior that was available in the sport coupe and sport sedan. Nicely designed bright aluminum end panels were a classy touch in finishing the seat cushion and seatback areas.

As in the past, the Super Sport interior offered bucket seats and a console. The center console was redesigned and included a rally-type clock. Accelerator, brake, and clutch pedals were trimmed with bright metal. Special attention to the instrumentation in the SS models eliminated the idiot lights in favor of real gauges for oil, temperature, amperage, and vacuum. A tachometer remained optional equipment. Exterior features included SS wheel covers, deep grille styling, and SS identification badges. Only the sport coupe and convertible were available with the SS package. The Impala models included the sport coupe, convertible, four-door sedan, four-door sport sedan (hardtop), and six- and nine-passenger station wagons. Four out of every ten Impalas built during this record-breaking year were Super Sports, an indicator of how much value Impala buyers placed on the car's sportiness and distinction.

A Higher Level of Luxury: Caprice

Notwithstanding the unmatched success enjoyed by the Impala brand, Chevrolet pushed for ways to raise the bar higher. Additional performance was available with the new 396-ci engine, a hard-charging motor that became a street warrior from the day it was introduced. But proving Chevy supremacy on the street and strip with the still-growing Impala was beginning to be a mismatch. The lighter, sportier Chevelle was a better home for the 396 when it came to grudge racing. Impalas were racing on pride and being driven by traditionalists. To stay on top of that game, bigger was no longer better, and lighter was a brighter idea. A 396 Impala in fine tune could still raise some hell, but the Chevelle performance advantage was just beginning to gather momentum. Enthusiastic Chevy drivers who went to war each weekend to uphold the pride of the bow tie saw the Impala being pushed aside. The Super Sport option, once an Impala exclusive, had been passed along to the Chevelle and Chevy II. The glory days of the Impala Super Sports had not yet faded over the horizon, but it was getting near sundown.

In terms of sheer numbers, people were drawn to the Impala for its good looks rather than its high-performance capabilities. And in this realm, the Impala was still the king. Chevrolet played the luxury card and upped the wager by making the Impala ever more like a baby Cadillac. In the middle of the 1965 production run, Chevrolet introduced the most luxurious car it ever built. It was hard to argue with the idea. Impala—the highest measure of a Chevy—was the big-time sales leader and Chevrolet couldn't

help but notice the enthusiastic practice of adding personal custom touches.

By noting the increasing demand for nicely equipped four-door Impalas, and the buyers' propensity to add optional comfort and convenience features, Chevrolet created the Caprice Custom Sedan. When it debuted (at the Chicago Auto Show in early 1965), Caprice was a one-model-only, special-edition sport sedan—a luxuriously appointed Impala four-door hardtop.

To set it apart from the standard Impala sport sedan—a model that was selling very well in its own regard—the Caprice sport sedan took to the highway with upgraded interior materials for seats, door panels, and headliners. Like cars with much higher price tags, it was trimmed with genuine wood rather than imitation wood grain. It also received extra touches such as a center armrest for rear-seat passengers, additional courtesy lamps, a special steering wheel, bright-metal door locks and turn-signal lever, plus the always important emblems and identification, which represented the exclusivity that was expected in a more prestigious vehicle. Outside, the rear cove area trim piece was identical to the SS trim, but it carried the Caprice name. The grille was also in the SS (blacked-out) style, but with the Caprice badge in place. Along with the visual attention to finer details, the suspension was notably softened for that big-car ride. The new Impala Caprice was all about sporty elegance. The combination not only proved to be successful, it set even higher expectations for full-size Chevrolets.

New for 1966 was the 427-ci big block. The engine was offered in factory-rated 390- and 425-horsepower versions. Additional V-8 engine options included the 396, 327, and 283. *Zone Five Photo*

Below the surface, the 1965 Chevy was finally able to shed the seven-year-old X-member frame. The new replacement was a full-perimeter frame that Chevy called Girder Guard. It utilized full-length side rails joined laterally by four cross-members. A redesigned coil-spring independent front suspension up front and a link-type coil rear suspension provided some improvement to maneuverability and level cornering. The wheels were also moved outward—2 inches in front and 3 inches in the rear—to aid cornering and provide a wider stance.

Paint choices included 13 new colors out of a total of 15 options, plus 9 two-tone possibilities. The acrylic lacquer process, known as Magic Mirror finish, was noted for its resistance to chipping, fading, and the corrosive effects of road tar and salt. Impalas and Super Sports were offered in 3 unique colors: Glacier Gray, Crocus Yellow, and Evening Orchid. Sport coupes and sport sedans could be ordered with black vinyl roofs.

Coming out of the blocks in 1965, the engine choices were nearly the same as in 1964. Only the limited-production

425-horsepower 409 was absent. Top power from a factory-built 409 was now rated at 400 horsepower. By midyear the remaining 409s were also dropped. This was the end of a legendary engine—one of the most desirable from the Impala's days of preeminence—but the beginning for an engine that would be smoother and equally powerful. Published reports indicate fewer than 3,000 full-size Chevys packed 409s in 1965.

The 409 was taken to its limits before it was retired. The promise of the new 396-ci engine was as big as the great outdoors. Performance and flexibility were its hallmarks. Although smaller in cubic-inch displacement, the high-performance version of the 396 was rated at 425 horsepower, the same as the 1964-issue, dual-quad 409. The big-horse 396 had the advantage of a forged crankshaft and pistons, four-bolt main bearings, a solid-lifter camshaft, larger intake valves, a large Holley four-barrel carb, and an aluminum manifold. Even in its more commonly seen 325-horse setup, the engine was still a mighty performer.

The 195-horsepower 283-ci engine with a three-speed manual transmission was standard in the Impala. Overdrive was optional on this configuration, as it was on the six-cylinder with three-speed option. Three-speed transmissions were also available on the 250- and 300-horsepower 327-ci engines. A four-speed manual was optional with any engine except the six, and the two-speed automatic Powerglide—the most popular transmission selection—was optional with all engines except the 400-horsepower 409.

Also introduced was the long-awaited option to the old Powerglide two-speed automatic—the three-speed Turbo Hydra-Matic 400, which was only available with the 325-horsepower 396 engine.

For years, Chevrolet treated buyers with an expansive list of optional equipment. Much of it—like the power accessories—comprised factory options for those who special ordered their cars. Other items were dealer add-ons. Judging by the number of customers who took advantage of these accessories, there was assuredly a willing and enthusiastic market for upscale Chevrolets. One magazine advertisement from 1965 made note of "nearly 200 custom touches . . . to make the Impala Super Sport as unique and personal as you like."

Introduction of the 396 Engine

Horsepower	Bore & Stroke	Crankshaft	Valvetrain	Compression	Carburetor
325 hp 4.00	4x3.76	cast steel	hydraulic	10:1	small 4 barrel
425 hp 4.00	4x3.76	forged steel	solid lifters	11:1	large 4 barrel

Inside the Super Sport, the bucket seats and a console were reminiscent of SS tradition. One particularly nice feature was the return of truly important gauges for oil, temperature, and amperage. They were attractively clustered on the forward portion of the console. *Zone Five Photo*

If customers were inclined to dress up their Impalas, why not provide some of the most popular accessories as a package? Chevy had great success doing this with the Super Sports, and patterned a luxury car version after that success—the Caprice.

Caprice became a separate model rather than an Impala trim level when the 1966 models were announced, officially displacing the Impala as the cream of the Chevrolet crop. From the one-and-only Caprice sport sedan in 1965, Chevrolet added a sport coupe and two station wagons in 1966.

And for those who thought the fastback-style roofline introduced in 1965 was too flashy for a luxury car, the new Caprice custom coupe reverted to a more formal, squared-off style. The Impala sport coupe retained the sleeker sport roof design. As part of the mystique associated with Caprice ownership, the car possessed a unique look, a heavier frame and suspension tweaks for an improved ride, and the more luxurious interior accouterments.

Minor evolutionary changes marked the Chevrolet redesign from 1965 to 1966. One of the more controversial aspects was the elimination of the three round taillight theme. Because that was an Impala trademark, and the Impala was losing its top-of-the-line status, it may have been a timely omission. For 1966 each taillight was a long, horizontal rectangular fixture that slightly wrapped around the rear of the car to provide some side lighting. Each unit

was divided into triple segments, a mindful reflection of Impala history and Chevrolet identity.

As with most face-lift redesigns, the fenders, bumpers, and grille received minor alterations. The redesign left Impala with a more massive appearance, suitable to pursuing the goals of luxury at a low cost. The trim-free side panels that were a noticeable improvement on 1965 Super Sports once again wore a long, narrow side spear.

Inside, the improvements included a slim seatback design that initiated the term *Strato* into the language of Chevy fans. Strato bucket seats and Strato bench seats were very popular in the sporty SS models. Needle gauges for oil pressure, temperature, and amperage were omitted from the standard SS package, but—like the tachometer—were still available as options.

Chevy continued its efforts to keep the interest of street-racing fanatics in 1966 with the introduction of the 427-ci L-72 engine. Although it was given the same 425-horsepower rating as the heavyweight 396 from 1965, it muscled up with an added 45 foot-pounds of torque. This factory-built, speed-shop engine came with a high-rise aluminum intake and a Holley four-barrel carburetor, a solid-lifter cam, oversize valves, forged aluminum pistons, and a forged steel crank. This most potent of engines was designed for racing, and therefore, didn't find its way into many Impalas. The king of the full-size Chevys was just too heavy for the meanest of mean streets or the strip.

The crossed flags with 427 identification on the front fenders did not go unnoticed on the street, and neither did this car's performance. Simulated wire wheels and spinners were optional equipment.
Zone Five Photo

Most of Chevy's performance buyers were shifting gears in the lighter, faster Chevelle with the big-block 396. And others who were looking for Chevy budget performance were turning their glances toward the sexy little Nova. But that didn't slow down the Impala's popularity as a sporty full-size car. It simply removed it from the racers' weapons-of-choice list. Impala was still in command of Chevy sales, and its Super Sport models remained far more popular than the SS versions in the Chevelle and Nova models. The Super Sports' image was craftily built around the lure of speed and danger, but in fact always had more to do with a preference than performance—preference for bucket seats, a console, a floor-mounted shifter, and a vinyl interior. Blowing the doors off all comers was the sweet reward of the hi-po guys who flaunted the most rare and most powerful best-of-breed big dogs.

When it came to overall success and sales, the Impala was still running away with all the awards. Certainly the

Super Sport Chevelles were capturing the high-performance enthusiasts who before the advent of intermediate-size cars were interested in Impala high performance. But buyers who desired and could afford more than a compact or intermediate-size car still streamed into the Chevrolet dealerships to own and drive Impalas.

And on the other end of the scale, Caprice was definitely luring buyers who used to purchase a loaded Impala to get their fill of Chevy-style luxury. Still, with all the ground between high performance and pre-packaged luxury, the Impala name, with its wide choice of economy or performance engines, was still magical in the minds of many.

SS Impala Production

Year	Totals
1961	.453
1962	99,000
1963	153,000
1964	185,000
1965	243,000
1966	119,000

The first thing you notice about the rear of the 1966 Impala is the taillights. Every Impala, except the 1959, had six round taillights across the back. Although the six individual segments were still there, an Impala trademark was missing. *Zone Five Photo*

Luxury Takes the Lead over Performance

"Adversity has the effect of eliciting talents, which in prosperous circumstances would have lain dormant."

—Horace

From 1967 to 1971 the Chevy Impala grew bigger and heavier. No surprise there. That was always the Impala way. It only seemed more obvious during these years because there were more small cars on the road than ever before. This put the Impala in a different light. Young buyers wanted smaller and less expensive cars that fit in better with their lifestyles. They thought the Impala was huge, especially compared to the cars they preferred. Middle-aged and older people still liked big cars, and they could afford them, so they continued to buy Impalas. Chevy set out to make those people happy. They concentrated on making Impala an affordable luxury car.

Even though the Impala had always been a favorite family car for the majority of buyers, the dressed-up and

Impala sales continued to be strong in the early 1970s. Although it hasn't received its due credit, Impala sport coupes, like this one at the 1971 Chicago Auto Show, were more popular than the same model Caprice. *1978–1999 GM Corp. Used with permission of GM Media Archives*

The SS was still something special for the full-size Impala in 1967. In either convertible or sport coupe form there were still plenty of buyers who wouldn't have their Chevy any other way. Smaller, lighter Super Sports in the Chevelle lineup had become the darling of the all-out performance enthusiasts, but big and bold still held a great deal of appeal. *1978–1999 GM Corp. Used with permission of GM Media Archives*

powerfully equipped versions were the ones that created the stir. Critics may be quick to dismiss the Impalas of this vintage because they were neither the classiest nor the fastest horses in the Chevy stable, but wallets were still opening to pay for the privilege of driving one home. The numbers proved Impala was still the right car for the time.

For those who wanted the highest-caliber performance, Impala was not the weapon of choice. But it was no slouch either. Even hauling the extra weight of the full-size Chevrolet, the 396 or 427 engines had enough power to produce more than a modicum of respect.

As always there were more people who liked the look of performance than those who actually wanted to wring out every drop of that eye-watering appropriation. Either way, the smaller Chevys were the best way to go. The Impala sport coupe and convertible could easily make an old guy feel young. But with the Chevelle SS, the Nova SS, and the hot new Camaro luring the youth, Impalas—not even Super Sports—were not going to entice many young guys. The big Impalas just no longer had "The Look" of the young and the restless.

Still, for some enthusiasts Impala *was* the look they wanted. In 1967, Chevy still put together an impressive high-performance Impala Super Sport model: the SS427. It was a classic SS with 385 horsepower on call at the jab of the accelerator pedal. The SS427 stood out in a crowd. In addition to the standard list of SS fringe benefits, the SS427 possessed its own special items—specifically a domed hood with three imitation carburetor intakes highlighted by chrome plating. Without the 427, the other SS and Impala models had the standard hood with the single windsplit.

All SS427s wore special badges within the blacked-out grille, the front fenders, and the deck lid. They also came with redline tires mounted on 14x6-inch wheels, plus heavy-duty springs and shocks, and a large-diameter front stabilizer bar.

Super Sports—including the SS427—were freed from the standard Impala side trim, and made a better impression by including black-accented chrome molding on the rocker panels and lower rear quarter panels. They also took advantage of a unique grille with blacked-out vertical bars for a wide, linear appearance. In typical SS fashion, these models

On the assembly lines, in the dealerships, and on the highways, Impala remained the number one Chevrolet. The familiar egg-crate–style grille was once again a prominent feature on the Impala. *1978–1999 GM Corp. Used with permission of GM Media Archives*

also wore unique wheel covers and badges. All-vinyl, Strato-back bucket seats were standard and the center console was part of the package. Options included the full gauge package with tachometer, front disc brakes, and accent striping.

In addition to the 427 Turbo Jet engine, other power choices included the 325-horsepower 396 Turbo Jet, the 275-horsepower Turbo Fire 327, the 195-horsepower Turbo Fire 283, and the 155-horsepower Turbo Thrift six cylinder. Missing from the list, after an 11-year run, was the popular 283.

Comparing the 1967 Impala to the 1966, the new Impala looked longer and heavier—but in reality it wasn't. Through the years Chevy designers had successfully played this card over and over. The sport coupe fastback roofline, introduced in 1965, still figured prominently in the overall design. This one aspect made it easy to accentuate long and flowing lines. Chevy, as well as several other cars of this era, remained committed to the Coke-bottle rear quarter panels that gave the car a sexy shape.

With the intent to design a car that looked expensive, the bumpers once again gained depth and appeared more massive. In 1965 and 1966, the blade-like front bumper split the grille.

When redesigning the grille for 1967, a more obvious egg-crate pattern was used and the slightly hooded headlights were kept within the grille area rather than peaking out as before. On the leading edge of the front fenders, just outboard of the headlights and above the bumper end caps, was a design element reminiscent of the hidden headlight housings on the first-generation Buick Rivieras. For a more elegant style, Impala buyers could order fender lights in these housings. This one-year-only feature was standard in the Caprice. The design gave the front fenders an edginess that pushed them ahead of the grille area and accented the V-style front bumper and hood style that was first implemented in 1965.

The Impalas also wore a side trim piece low on the door, which also added to the visual effect that the car was heavier. The side trim connected the front and rear wheelwells just above the centerline of the wheels, then continued from the rear wheelwell to the rear bumper end cap. The traditional Chevy wheel openings that were flared on

As always, the Impala was built to provide more for the money than the competition offered. The standard V-8 was still the reliable 283, but options included the Turbo-Fire 327, Turbo-Jet 396, Turbo-Jet 427, and of course, the Turbo-Thrift six cylinder. *1978–1999 GM Corp. Used with permission of GM Media Archives*

the rearward edge and implied a sense of speed or performance gave way to a more formal appearance with the rear edge curving back toward the wheel. They also emphasized the roundness and the lowness of the design.

With the skillful application of several time-tested redesign methods, the Chevy designers completed a successful redesign that looked more conservative and more luxurious.

The Impala owner could add to this by visiting the option list and selecting items normally associated with Cadillac and other luxury cars: six-way power seats, power windows, air conditioning, 8-track stereo tape system, Comfortilt steering wheel, and Strato-back or Strato-bucket front seats. And that was just the short list.

The taillight treatment in 1967 more clearly identified the six individual taillight theme popularized by Impala through 1965. Although still a one-piece design as on the 1966, brightwork clearly divided the fixture into thirds. The lights rode above the rear bumper within a black-finished cove, and were connected by a trim strip that was bright on the Impalas and a linear, black and bright combination on the SS Impalas and the Caprice.

Some say that when Caprice became the icing on the full-size Chevy cake, Impala lost its luxury image. But all was not lost. The Impala was many things to many people, not the least of which was plenty of car for the money. It may not have been as high-performance as it once was, but it was still strong enough for all but the most unrestrained drivers. It was no longer the most luxurious of Chevys, but it had enough to please a healthy portion of discriminating Chevy buyers.

Impala had a very popular sport coupe, but its once-powerful performance image had been undercut, most notably by Chevelle, and to a lesser extent by Nova and the new Camaro. Impala was really more of a luxury car, but Caprice had a lock on the only two-door, formal-style, hardtop coupe—a popular body style of that time. In addition to the rakish sport coupe, Impala offered a sport sedan (four-door hardtop), a four-door sedan, a convertible, and two station wagons. The distinction between Impala and the Bel Air and Biscayne continued to be seen in bright moldings and accent trim, emblems, interior fabrics, and the likelihood of Impala buyers accessorizing from the substantial list of options.

Safety was a major issue in 1967, as the cadence of consumerism caused auto manufacturers to walk to the beat of a different drummer. Accident avoidance features such as windshield washers and two-speed wipers became

The Impala sport coupe for 1968 continued with the long, fastback-style roofline that was first introduced in 1965, but the more formal custom coupe was also added. Also returning was the full-length side molding. *1978–1999 GM Corp. Used with permission of GM Media Archives*

The roofline of the four-door sport sedan was not as streamlined as the sport coupe, but not as upright as the custom coupe. And look what's back—six round taillights. Just like old times again. *1978–1999 GM Corp. Used with permission of GM Media Archives*

An Impala custom coupe nears the end of the assembly line in 1969. Notice the bow-tie logo in the center of the grille. Thirty years later the Impala will have changed dramatically, but the bow tie in front will be the same. *1978–1999 GM Corp. Used with permission of GM Media Archives*

standard equipment, as did anti-glare mirrors and improved brakes. Passenger safety improvements included padded instrument panels and sun visors. Rear-seat passengers could buckle up just like the front-seat occupants. And controls for the accessory items were redesigned to be less dangerous should someone forcefully contact them in an accident. This was just the beginning, as safety concerns would become increasingly important.

1968 Impala

The Impala luxury image was doubtlessly enhanced with the addition of the custom coupe model in 1968. Across the board, the popularity of two-door hardtops was conspicuous. Impala's fastback-style sport coupe was a popular car, but it created somewhat of an identity crisis. Impala was banking on customers who preferred a more traditional, more conservative appearance. Maybe a little more Main Street than Monte Carlo. For those who might,

in fact, want Monte Carlo, Chevy had something in the works. For the time being, Impala would take the high road of luxury over sportiness.

The custom coupe was a two-door hardtop with a formal (squared-off) roofline, certainly a more buttoned-down style compared to the fastback roofline of the sport coupe. Impala—still the undisputed favorite of mainstream Americans, especially in its four-door sedan variant—once again was identifying itself more with Cadillac than Corvette. One year earlier the custom coupe body style had been an exclusive of the upscale Caprice. For those who thought Caprice to be slightly more extravagant than necessary, Impala was still the all-American choice.

Comparing the Caprice and the Impala, Caprice maintained its level of distinctive touches. One item was the side trim treatment. The 1968 Impala's side trim was higher on the side of the car, lining up with the top of the headlights and the top of the rear bumper, and passing clos-

The redesign of the 1969 Impala resulted in a unique, one-year-only front end that enclosed the grille within a heavy bumper that included vertical elements on each end and a wide trim strip beneath the leading edge of the hood. *1978–1999 GM Corp. Used with permission of GM Media Archives*

er to the door handle than the tops of the wheelwells. Compared to the Caprice, which was styled with a lower side trim, the Impala sport coupe looked lighter, while the formal Caprice coupe looked much heavier and more in keeping with its luxurious intent.

Compared to the 1967 Impala models, the 1968 design was more refined. Most obvious was the reintroduction of the thin, blade-style front bumper, which split the grille. The bumper also connected two vertical bumper elements that took the form of the front fenders. As in 1967, the leading edges of the front fenders played a strong role in the front-end design. However, in the 1968 redesign their role was more proportionate. In particular, the decorative grille work above the bumper end caps was nicely integrated into the design. Overall the Impala front end still resembled the classic 1963–1965 Buick Riviera, a car

Even though Caprice was established as the luxury car in the Chevrolet lineup, Impala still offered the only convertible. The successful debut of the Monte Carlo took the spotlight in 1970, but if you want a collectible Chevy from this year, you're looking at it. *1978–1999 GM Corp. Used with permission of GM Media Archives*

The V-style front bumper, which came on the scene in 1965, is clearly seen in this photo of a 1970 Impala four-door sport sedan. Also note the hidden windshield wipers, a feature that was first implemented in 1968. *1978–1999 GM Corp. Used with permission of GM Media Archives*

that was known for its fusion of sportiness and elegance. Hidden headlights, another of the Riviera's recognizable features, became an option on the Caprice for 1968.

Impala was redirecting its performance orientation along the lines of a European touring car rather than a drag-racing icon. The Impala Super Sports were still on hand to make sure the marque didn't relinquish its sporty flair entirely. But as an indicator of where this was headed, after a four-year run as a series separate from the Impala, the Super Sports were once again handled as an option package.

Dressing up an Impala with options was still a popular pastime. The list of factory and dealer accessories was substantial. However, the trends with late-1960s Impala owners indicated the add-ons were more frequently conveniences and luxuries rather than performance enhancements.

The Super Sport package remained a popular option, but not like it once was when Impala was the darling of a more youthful group of owners. For those who still wanted an Impala that could kick some butt, there was the SS427, a mean—if not lean—driving machine. To distinguish it from the less muscular SS cars, it once again wore unique SS427 badges, a blacked-out grille, a special domed hood, redline tires on 15x6-inch wheels, and was outfitted with the heavy-duty suspension equipment. This was a fire-breathing throw-back to the original SS in 1961, which also was a full-bore performance package.

The standard SS package could be added to the sport coupes and convertibles with any engine option the buyer desired. As tradition would have it, this option brought with it the usual SS badges modified somewhat from the

previous year, special wheel covers, and the Strato bucket-seat interior with a console.

Chevy also started organizing non-SS options into complementary groups. Some items in a group could be ordered separately, others were only available as a group. For example, the Decor Group was comprised of a deluxe oval steering wheel, rear fender skirts, and bright-metal molding for the roof, door, and window frames. The Appearance Guard Group included deluxe front and rear seat belts, door-edge guards, front and rear rubber-faced bumper guards, and front and rear rubber floor mats. Eventually the opportunity for completely individual customization would give way to the prepackaged groups.

Many Chevy fans would miss it, but the 283 was finally replaced by the 307, essentially a 283 with a longer stroke. The bore was identical to the old engine, but changes included a new cylinder head, a different connecting-rod assembly, and some minor casting changes. It shared a crankshaft with the base 327 engine, and retained the camshaft and valvetrain from the 283. The 307 and base 327 made use of two-barrel Rochester carburetors. The Rochester Quadra-Jet was fueling the top-performing 327, the 396, and the tamer version of the 427.

Engine choices overall remained plentiful for the Impalas and other full-size Chevys. The economy-minded opted for a 155-horsepower 250-ci six. Five V-8 choices began with the 200-horse 307, and progressed to 250- and 275-horse 327s, the 325-horse 396, and 385- and 425-horse 427s. Although the 350-ci engine was being used in Camaros and Chevy IIs and a 350- and 375-horse 396

could be ordered into Chevelles and Camaros, none of those engines were options for Impala. Certainly there was no shortage of choices, but the performance orientation was geared toward a highway cruiser and capable road car.

Transmission options included Powerglide, Turbo Hydra-Matic, plus three- and four-speed manuals. A new stirrup-style shift lever (like an inverted U) was a cool addition to Impalas (Chevelles and Camaros, too) with floor-mounted consoles. The shift lever was a good fit for all but the most ham-handed drivers and featured a shift detent bar on the underside of the hand-grip area. The manually operated reverse gear lockout on four-speed transmissions was replaced by a simple spring-resistance security lockout.

It may not grab your attention immediately, but after you notice the windshield wipers are hidden on the 1968 Impala it becomes a significant feature. Without the wipers lying open on the windshield, the unobstructed line from hood to windshield added a new dimension of sleekness to the overall design. The cowl vent grille—between the base of the windshield and the hood—was eliminated by lengthening and elongating the hood. When the wipers are not in use, the wiper arms are recessed below a slightly forward reveal molding.

The instrument panel on the 1968 Impala and other full-size Chevys was completely restyled. The speedometer was centered and a clock mounted to the right. The typical assortment of warning lights was positioned below and within the speedometer head. When the special-order

To illustrate the changes from 1970 to 1971, and also put Caprice in the spotlight, Chevrolet photographed a basic 1970 Impala custom coupe next to a 1971 Caprice custom coupe. This was obviously not done to boost Impala sales. *1978–1999 GM Corp. Used with permission of GM Media Archives*

1967 the taillights were located within the bumper.

Interior features that separated Impalas from the other full-size Chevys, as well as from the competition, included upgraded upholstery and patterned vinyl headliners. Although these interiors were not as distinctive as the interiors of the early Impala models, they remained a noticeable upgrade from the choices afforded to Bel Air and Biscayne buyers.

The choices for exterior paint included 15 solid colors, plus 6 two-tone combinations. Impala sport sedans and sport coupes had a vinyl roof option in either black or white. And convertible tops came in white, black, and blue.

Topping the list of frequently selected optional equipment were items like power disc brakes; power seats, door locks, and windows; air conditioning; seat belts; head restraints; AM-FM stereo radio; and power antenna. A new collective of options was marketed as the Operating Convenience Group. It included an electric clock, remote-control outside mirror, and rear-window defroster.

Astro ventilation improved the air flow/air distribution ducting fresh air to both ends of the instrument panel and creating a system that circulated fresh air more efficiently and with better control. The cowl kick-panel vents, formerly the only fresh air vents, remained and were operated independently. Astro ventilation was an option on the entire Chevrolet lineup, except the Caprice coupe where it was standard.

1969 Impala

The redesign for 1969 eliminated the fastback coupe from the Chevy model lineup. The sleek sport coupe roofline was replaced by a more moderate roofline. Although not as conservative as the custom coupe, this new look for the sport coupe signaled a further erosion of Impala's sporty image, which had been fading since the introduction of the intermediate-size Chevelle. The performance banner was handed over to Chevelle, Nova, and Camaro, as the Impala's role as an enthusiast's car shriveled to almost embarrassing proportions. But don't confuse that assessment with an extensive lack of enthusiasm for the Impala. Just the opposite was true; sales were outstanding.

Chevrolet made some momentous changes in the decade of the 1960s. When the decade began Chevrolet was just introducing a second line of cars, the Corvair, for a mass market. Impala was clearly the performance and luxury leader of the Chevy lineup. (Excluding Corvette because it was a different product, for a different customer, and at a different price.) By the end of the decade, Chevy was producing six passenger-car models. Full-size models,

gauge package was chosen, a tachometer slipped into the gas-gauge space, and gauges for the oil pressure, gas, temperature and amp meters were set into the speedometer head. All the control knobs were bigger and flatter, a concession to the safety standards that were being emphasized. Outside, marker lights on the four corners of the car became an industry standard.

In typical fashion, the upscale Impala received appearance extras that separated it from Biscayne and Bel Air: rocker panel moldings, front and rear wheelwell opening trim, door and window bead trim moldings, end panels on the front seats, a classier steering wheel, and the ever popular three-unit taillight configuration. Although not quite round, these taillights easily identified an Impala. As in

With a vinyl roof and full wheel covers, this 1970 Impala custom coupe can hold its own against more expensive cars. The 350-ci engine was standard. *1978–1999 GM Corp. Used with permission of GM Media Archives*

which were 80 percent of all cars sold 10 years earlier, were reduced to about 40 percent by 1970. Despite those watershed changes, Impalas remained the king of the hill. Basically, it could be summed up by saying the Impala was safer, more comfortable, and a more desirable symbol of success than all the small cars that had come on the scene.

The full-size Chevrolet's styling evolution from 1968 to 1969 was without startling changes. The face-lift included a new "loop-style" front bumper. Chevrolet noted the one-piece bumper design provided greater strength and rigidity. Although the bumper design continued to display a slight V-shaped nose in the center and each fender pushed the bumper outward on each end, the bumper imparted a bulldozer-like appearance to the front end. Because Chevy continued to push around the competition when it came to sales, the bumper was appropriately symbolic. It surrounded a traditional Chevy egg-crate–style grille and quad headlights. The openings between the grille bars were considerably smaller than those used in the 1968 Impala grille. A Chevy bow-tie logo was prominently displayed in the center of the main grille. Adding to the prominence of the front-end design, Chevrolet designers allowed about one-quarter of the grille to peak out below the front bumper. The split-grille theme had been a popular Impala design trait dating back to 1965.

A new hood extended to the top of the bumper. The header panel used in 1968 was eliminated. The Chevrolet name was spelled out in individual letters across the leading edge of the hood on Impalas. As part of the redesign, the front fender moldings, wheel opening moldings, nameplates, emblems, and engine designation plates were all new.

Around behind, the Impala once again featured three individual taillights embedded in each side of a plank-like rear bumper. In a break from tradition, however, the lights were rectangular rather than rounded.

Side panels were designed with subtle bulges around the wheelwells. These contours to an otherwise almost slab-sided body hinted at the fender lines and conformation of the Chevrolets from the early 1950s. The sheet metal behind the front wheelwells, including the forward section of the door panels, appeared slightly inflated. A similar effect was used ahead of and above the rear wheelwells. As a result the Impalas had a heavier, more substantial, and more Cadillac-like character. With the formal coupe roofline and fender skirts, the Impala could easily be mistaken for a more expensive automobile.

One year after Chevrolet dropped the old, reliable 283 V-8, it said good-bye to another classic small block, the 327. In its place was the 350. Frame, suspension, and drive line remained essentially the same as for the 1968 Impala.

The SS427 was back. And for the first time since 1961 an SS wasn't limited to a sport coupe or convertible. The Impala custom coupe was the new addition. Depending on the customer's performance expectations, the 427 could be configured to deliver 335, 390, or 425 horsepower. Identifying SS badges were located on the front quarter panels below the full body length trim, rearward of the top of the front wheelwell and just ahead of the leading edge of the door. Badges were also placed in the center of the grille and center of the deck lid. Inside, the only SS marker was in the center of the steering wheel.

1970 Impala

When the spotlight was flipped on in 1970, the center of attention was a two-door coupe. It was reminiscent of 1958 when the Impala first burst out of the gate. Only this year it wasn't the Impala.

The successful formula that previously worked magic for Impala cast a spell this time around in the name of Monte Carlo. In 1958, Chevrolet used the term *executive coupe* as a description of the new Impala. In 1970 the term *personal luxury car* was in vogue. Regardless of the semantics, the Monte Carlo was successful because it was so much like that original Impala. It was that perfect blend of sportiness and elegance, a key ingredient in the original Impala sport coupes and also in the original Buick Riviera.

Bill Mitchell, Chuck Jordan, and many other GM designers who were influenced by Harley Earl had a talent for this sort of thing. Like the successful Impalas of the 1960s, the Monte Carlo relied on the flavor of Cadillac to develop an air of prestige.

Although it was not as large as the 1970 Impala, the Monte Carlo had a big-car appearance. Its unmistakable characteristic was a 6-foot-long hood. No other Chevy ever matched it. Yet the overall proportions of the Monte Carlo were handsome and chiseled. In its standard form, Monte Carlo offered considerable luxury for the price, which was slightly less than $3,000. For a few more bucks, a more enthusiastic driver could replace the basic-issue 350-ci engine with the highly potent 454. Monte Carlo sales were sensational from day one. It quickly rose to become Chevy's single most popular model for most of the next 10 years. Unlike the Impala, the Monte Carlo never was offered in another body style. Monte Carlo remained a two-door coupe.

Despite being moved off center stage, the Impala continued to hold its own when it came to sales. The intermediate-size Chevelle and the smaller Chevrolets such as Nova and Camaro were popular, but not the answer for everyone. And likewise the upscale Caprice remained a hit, but there was still plenty of room for Impala to maneuver. Impala still offered five separate body styles (four-door sedan and four-door hardtop, two-door sport coupe and two-door custom coupe, and convertible) whereas the other full-size Chevy nameplates only offered two each.

Clearly Impala's place was secure, even if its vitality wasn't what it once was.

In 1970, Impala received the usual face-lift, which resulted in minor changes to the front, rear, and sides. The heavy-looking loop-style bumper, with the massive vertical supports on either end, was replaced with a more traditional bumper with to the split-grille theme. And the leading edge of the front fenders was squared off so they no longer played a dominant role in front-end design. The bumper curled around the front fenders as was commonly seen on Impalas prior to 1967.

The rear of the car was also squared off compared to the 1969 model, and the rear bumper was slightly wider, flatter, and more substantial. The three distinctive taillights on each side were once again recessed within the bumper, but this time the style was done in vertical rectangles.

A new big-block V-8 was introduced in 1970—the 454. Two variants were available: one rated at 345 horsepower and the other at 390. Next in line was the 300-horsepower 350 and a 265-horsepower 400-ci engine. These were all considered optional engines, with the 307 remaining the basic mill. The 427 and the four-speed manual transmission were relegated to history. The three-speed manual, the three-speed Turbo Hydra-Matic automatic transmission, and the two-speed Powerglide automatic continued to fill the bill.

If you ordered the Impala custom coupe, it was outfitted with front disc brakes (also standard on the Caprice), but other Impalas were equipped with drum brakes on all four wheels.

CHAPTER 7

Less Credit Than It Deserves

"The best way to have a good idea is to have lots of ideas."

—Linus Pauling

Little has been written about the Chevy Impala in the post-musclecar era. And nearly all of what has made it into books describes the car in unflattering terms. It would be easy to believe the Impala became the Edsel of the 1970s and 1980s. But the facts speak a different story. Impala sales remained strong. And strong is really too mild a term. The impression that the top-of-the-line Caprice was more popular than the Impala is wrong. In a head-to-head comparison for the years 1972 through 1976, the Impala easily outsold its Caprice counterpart. The Chevelle Malibu gets credit for being a much sportier car than the Impala, but which car sold more convertibles during this era? The Impala. The lower-priced Malibu sold more hardtop coupes than Impala, but not by a wide margin.

In 1972, Chevrolet built the 10 millionth Impala. It took a little more than 14 years to set that amazing record.

Few changes were made as the Impala cruised from 1971 into 1972. The all-time best Chevrolet theme song—"See the USA in Your Chevrolet"—made a return visit with a little twist: "Building a Better Way to See the USA." *1978–1999 GM Corp. Used with permission of GM Media Archives*

A milestone was reached during the 1972 model year when the 10 millionth Impala was built. No other car ever climbed that mountain before or since. At this point in its history, the Impala had been designed to provide low-cost luxury. *1978–1999 GM Corp. Used with permission of GM Media Archives*

Don't bother going to the books to find another model that can match that number. Nothing else comes close. Remember, this isn't the total number of Chevrolets built. It's Impalas only. Ten million families took home brand-new Impalas during that time. Imagine how many more families bought used Impalas at that time. And then how many went to multiple homes. And how many first-time Impala owners became second- and third-time owners. This is the giant redwood of family trees. And it's still growing.

Stories of the Impala's demise were greatly exaggerated. The enthusiast press never grasped the concept that the Impala continued to excel at what it always did best—giving people what they wanted in a car. Unfortunately the press clippings for this type of achievement don't make a very tall stack, and Chevys that don't smoke their tires aren't found on the covers of many magazines or in the pages of many books. Conversely, those that do aren't within shouting distance of the Impala's sales records.

As the Impala headed into the era when smog controls, safety, and fuel economy became important considerations for designing cars, and purchasing them, the auto industry

in general was scrambling to adjust. Imports were making real strides in the areas of economy, reliability, and quality. There were some difficult lessons being learned in Detroit. Yet through it all, where did more American buyers turn to get the car they really wanted? They went to their local Chevy dealer and bought an Impala.

The four-door sedan was the most popular choice, but it just barely surpassed the custom coupe, which remained a favorite choice for Impala buyers in 1972. Right behind those models was the four-door hardtop. Stylish and practical—Impala was still doing it better than anyone.

In terms of outward appearance, the Impala showed only small changes from 1971. The emphasis continued to be on luxury, and the resemblance to Cadillac remained a fundamental connection for the Impala image.

It should also be noted that when making performance comparisons between the 1972 and newer Impalas with the 1971 and older Impalas there were new methods of determining horsepower ratings. The 1972 and newer cars were rated on net horsepower rather than gross horsepower, which resulted in significantly lower numbers. However,

The Impala hardtop sedan came within a shadow of being the top-selling Impala during 1972. Production totals topped 170,000, a few thousand shy of the four-door sedan, and almost 100,000 more than the comparable Caprice. *1978–1999 GM Corp. Used with permission of GM Media Archives*

the 365-horsepower 454-ci engine from 1971 delivered the same real-world performance as the 270-horsepower 454 from 1972. The horsepower race that was a badge of courage during the late 1950s and all through the 1960s was over, but the advertised ratings are often misunderstood when the change from gross to net is not taken into consideration.

The original Chevy 265-ci, small-block V-8 grew to 400 ci by 1973, a measure of the trend toward bigger, more luxurious Chevrolets. Another sign of the times: the Impala convertible was history. Put it in the books. The 6,456 built in 1972 marked the end of an era. Caprice got the pleasure of offering the drop-top option in 1973 and managed to sell 7,339. On the big scorecard, however, Impala easily outsold Caprice in every comparable model. Throughout the Chevy lineup the hardtop coupe continued its pattern of sales success. Impala outsold Malibu, but the Monte Carlo took over the role of most popular two-door coupe in the Chevy family. Missing from the family photo in 1973 was the Impala's

Without the Chevy bow tie and the nameplate in the grille, this 1972 Impala hardtop coupe could pass for a more expensive, upscale automobile. The Impala mission was to deliver Cadillac dreams on a Chevy budget. *1978–1999 GM Corp. Used with permission of GM Media Archives*

In 1963 and 1964, Impala convertible production topped 80,000. In 1972 the total was less than 6,500. Even at that, Impala convertibles outnumbered the Malibu drop-tops. *1978–1999 GM Corp. Used with permission of GM Media Archives*

plain-Jane sibling, the Biscayne. Its 14-year run from 1959 was brought to an end without fanfare—an unheralded car that sold and performed well outside of the limelight.

Changes to the Impala between 1972 and 1976 were minimal. Performance orientation was sidetracked while items such as pollution and safety took center stage. Engines designed to run cleaner didn't create the same excitement as engines designed to go faster. Bumpers designed to absorb impacts never were admired like those designed to deliver impact. And as the popularity of small cars increased, the Impala looked increasingly out of place and out of touch with what most people wanted. Although production of full-size cars decreased substantially, Impala sales continued their substantial lead over Caprice. Sales of Impala sport coupes and custom coupes outpaced Malibu. But the combination of an industry-wide sales slump and a market that was quickly shifting to smaller cars put the future of full-size Chevrolets in a dilemma. Impala always sold more four-door sedans than any other body style during the 1972–1976 period. In 1972 sedan production was nearly 185,000, but by 1976 that figure had skidded to

At first glimpse 1973 Impala sales were far off the record-setting years of 1963 through 1965, but Chevrolet was producing a lot more models than it had been 10 years earlier. The best-selling Impala was the four-door sedan, but close behind was the custom coupe. Overall, Impala was clearly more popular than the upscale Caprice. *1978–1999 GM Corp. Used with permission of GM Media Archives*

On the test track the 1974 Impala made a splash. Improvements were made in safety and emissions control, but the U.S. economy was sluggish and industry-wide car sales were down. Impala did not buck that trend. *1978–1999 GM Corp. Used with permission of GM Media Archives*

86,000. Even the hot new Monte Carlo hardtop coupe, which had been selling like hot dogs on the Fourth of July, had a bite taken out of its sales streak by 1975.

In an attempt to package Impalas differently and create some exclusivity, Chevrolet introduced, in 1974, a limited-edition "Spirit of America" Impala, painted white with red and blue accent stripes and special wheels. America's bicentennial was drawing near, so Chevrolet along with everyone else dipped their product in patriotic colors hoping to attract attention. It didn't get much. In 1975 another attempt to cash in on a trend brought forth the landau coupe. The two-door coupe was still popular, and the landau roof (thickly padded vinyl covering only the rear passenger area) sold relatively well on Chevelles and Monte Carlos. On Impalas it was not as hot. In its first season, less than 2,500 Impala landau coupes were sold. After several years in production and sales that never managed to nudge far above the 10,000-unit mark, the landau coupe was dropped. When white belts and shoes become popular again, these low-production coupes will become collectors' items.

The Bel Air, for many years the finest Chevrolet made and then longtime second fiddle to Impala, was unceremoniously dropped from the Chevy listings after the 1975 model year. Some wondered aloud how long it would be before the same fate would befall the Impala.

Chevy introduced the mini-size Chevette in 1976, calling more attention to the awkwardness of a full-size car like Impala. But the end was not in sight. Not yet. A new Impala/Caprice was but one year away.

In order to get through 1976, Impala wore hand-me-down front-end styling from the 1975 Caprice. There was very little distinction between the two models at this point. While Impala popularity continued to decrease, Caprice enjoyed a bit of a surge. However, Impala maintained its sales leadership position over Caprice.

There was plenty of Cadillac flavor in the 1974 Impala. The big American family sedan was losing favor, and the designers were already at work on a dramatically smaller version that would be introduced three years into the future. *1978–1999 GM Corp. Used with permission of GM Media Archives*

Impala Production 1972-1976

1972
Four-door sedans	184,596
Four-door hardtop sedans	170,304
Convertibles	6,456
Hardtop coupes	52,692
Custom hardtop coupes	183,493

1973
Four-door sedans	190,536
Four-door hardtop sedans	139,143
No convertibles	
Hardtop coupes	42,979
Custom hardtop coupes	176,824

1974
Four-door sedans	133,164
Four-door hardtop sedans	76,492
No convertibles	
Sport coupes	50,036
Custom hardtop coupes	98,062

1975
Four-door sedans	91,330
Four-door hardtop sedans	47,125
No convertibles	
Sport coupes	21,333
Custom coupes	49,455
Landau coupes	2,465

1976
Four-door sedans	86,057
Four-door sport sedans	39,849
Impala S sport sedans	18,265
Impala wagons	40,986
Custom coupes	43,219
Impala Landau coupes	10,841

Four-door sedans were the Impala's bread and butter. The most common were the four-door models with a permanent pillar between the doors, but also available were a four-door hardtop (pillarless), and an S model sport sedan. In a very un-Impala-like fashion, Chevy eliminated the Impala sport coupe, a move that was interpreted by some as yet another indicator that the Impala was not long for this world.

Impala was rejuvenated in 1977 with a much-needed redesign. There hadn't been such a radical difference in two consecutive Impalas since 1959. The result was a car that, in its upscale Caprice trim, received the *Motor Trend* Car of the Year award. *Motor Trend*'s summation: "Chevrolet had simply put the act together in a harmonious whole that combined performance, economy, looks, comfort, and handling in one outstanding package that, on sum, outpointed everything else."

Compared to the 1977 Impalas, the Impalas of the late 1960s and early to mid-1970s might as well have been from an episode of the Flintstones. From longer, lower, and wider—Chevy convictions since the days of Harley Earl—to shorter, higher, and narrower, this wasn't just a new chapter for Chevrolet, it was a completely new book.

So dramatic was this downsizing that the 1977 midsize Malibu and Monte Carlo were bigger than the full-size Impalas and Caprices. A year later the midsize cars got their downsized redesign and order was restored. With the complete redesign it might have been easy for Chevrolet to retire

Impala offered a custom coupe (shown here) and a sport coupe in 1974. The custom proved to be more popular by a two-to-one margin. The Chevy factories rolled out nearly 100,000 custom coupes, while the four-door sedan topped the charts with more than 133,000 vehicles. *1978–1999 GM Corp. Used with permission of GM Media Archives*

The Impala landau coupe was a low-production car in 1976. Published reports indicate a total of 10,841 were built. In this last year of the big Impalas, overall production failed to reach 160,000. *1978–1999 GM Corp. Used with permission of GM Media Archives*

Before there were minivans, big sedans hauled around the kids and all their gear. The final year for the big Impala was 1976. A new day was coming and the Impala still had a big part to play. *1978–1999 GM Corp. Used with permission of GM Media Archives*

the Impala and introduce a new nameplate for the next generation of full-size Chevrolets. All those who had announced the passing of the Impala would have loved to take their bows and say "I told you so," but for 1977 the name lived on.

The new Impala was crisply styled and businesslike. It was a smack-on-the-forehead attention-getter for traditional Chevy buyers, but they loved it. It renewed their faith in Chevrolet and clearly showed the way for a new era in automobile design where bigger was not necessarily better. When the design team faced the challenges of the new 1977 Impala, it came down to some tough decisions. The goal was a smaller package than the year before. That wasn't a big problem. The most difficult aspect was providing more headroom, more trunk room, more sound insulation, more rear-seat legroom, more corrosion protection, more ease of entry and exit, and a car that was more manageable in traffic. And then there was the traditional Chevy mission: Build a car with some Cadillac flavor. Throughout the years there were times when the flavor was stronger than others, and 1977 was one of the flavorful years. For a lot of folks, it took a double-take to positively identify an Impala from a Cadillac Seville.

Chuck Jordan was the head of General Motors design studios during the development of the 1977 Impala/Caprice. His assessment, as reported by *Motor Trend,* was: "Someday I'm sure we'll look back at the '70s as an era of automotive styling at the crossroads. We believe the 1977 Chevrolet will set a new design standard in the automotive world through its pioneering styling efforts—one that the entire industry could well follow in the years to come. It's a dramatic turnabout in design."

He wasn't wrong about the rest of the industry following. The 1977 Impala/Caprice was a style leader. It wasn't sexy like a 1962 Impala Super Sport with a four speed and a 409, but this was the age of practicality. This was a car designed to appeal to the broad spectrum of buyers rather than the enthusiast appeal of the 1962 Impala SS. It was a complete repackaging, with very little in common with its previous model. In this regard, Impala went from zero to 100 in just one year. As Jordan aptly stated in the February 1977 *Motor Trend,* "The way things turned out, our design approach on this car couldn't have been more timely."

The model lineup was simplified: four-door sedan, two-door coupe, and four-door wagon. The base engine was the 250-ci six cylinder, with 305- and 350-ci V-8s as options. Those engines got one-, two-, and four-barrel carburetors respectively. For the likes of the *Motor Trend* test drivers, the most powerful engine and the optional F-41 suspension were definite pluses. The F-41 suspension consisted of heavy-duty springs and shock absorbers, a bigger anti-sway bar up front, and the inclusion of an anti-sway bar in the rear. According to *Motor Trend,* "This has to be the bargain of the century ($37), because it makes the Caprice handle like no other full-size sedan from Motor City. . . . To our way of thinking, it should be the first option specified by any buyer of a Caprice or Impala."

Although the idea hadn't caught on in the United States yet, a performance-equipped Impala was, in fact, an enthusiast's sedan. Certainly more so than the big, heavy Chevys from the previous five years. This car, even with less horsepower, could run circles around Chevys of the recent

The biggest story of the 1970s was the downsizing of the full-size Impala and Caprice in 1977. The midsize Chevys would get the same treatment one year later, but until then they were actually bigger than the traditional full-size Impala/Caprice. *1978–1999 GM Corp. Used with permission of GM Media Archives*

After the resized Impala and Caprice were introduced, Impala popularity increased dramatically. However, the Caprice took over the lead in that Chevy game of one-on-one. The four-door sedan model was the leader for both marques. In 1979, Caprice production exceeded 200,000, while Impala was just shy of 175,000. The Impala coupe (shown here), once a best-selling Chevy, had fallen to a limited production of 26,000. *1978–1999 GM Corp. Used with permission of GM Media Archives*

It was not a good year for the auto industry in 1980, and the Impala wasn't the only car to take a tumble. Sport coupe production dwindled to 10,000 and the mainstay four-door sedan only mustered 70,000. Caprice put up only slightly better numbers. *1978–1999 GM Corp. Used with permission of GM Media Archives*

past. About 700 pounds of ugly fat had been trimmed from the previous Impala (fat that chief engineer Thomas Zimmer said did not have anything to do), an exercise program that certainly aided performance. But this was still performance as defined within a nonperformance era. However, for the average car owner, this improvement in handling and versatile packaging was monumental; it didn't go unnoticed.

The new Impala/Caprice sedans were an immediate hit. After its first year, the Caprice supplanted the Olds Cutlass as the most popular model in America. In model-to-model comparisons, Caprice managed a slight lead over Impala, something that hadn't happened before. For a badge that some said had lost its juice, Impala put more than a quarter million cars on the road each year for three consecutive years: 1977, 1978, and 1979. Each year the

Impala hadn't changed appreciably since the redesign in 1977, but the market had. Four-door sedan production dropped from 197,000 to 60,000 for Impala and from 213,000 to 90,000 for Caprice. *1978–1999 GM Corp. Used with permission of GM Media Archives*

The good times for Impala were all in the past by 1981, a worse year than 1980. Not that Impala was alone as the curtain call was drawing nearer. The American car manufacturers were in a funk. Nothing was selling well, but smaller, more fuel-efficient cars were winning the war of attrition. Only 5,000 Impala sport coupes were built in 1981. *1978–1999 GM Corp. Used with permission of GM Media Archives*

Impala received moderate face-lifts—the typical changes such as redesigned grilles, taillights, interior trims, paint colors, and accessories—the types of things that Chevy, and all manufacturers, always did to distinguish one model year from the next.

With the U.S. economy sucking wind in 1980, every car manufacturer struggled to sell cars. Impala took a big hit, dropping production to just under 100,000 and sinking deeper in 1981. The upscale Caprice continued to outsell Impala, but the differences were small. Together they couldn't muster the sales that Impala alone had accomplished just a few years earlier.

The 305-ci V-8 engine featured an electronic spark control system that allowed the relatively high-compression engine to run on low-octane unleaded fuel. New technology was beginning to play a role at Chevrolet. In this case, a knock-sensor was used to signal a computer, which would then retard the spark whenever necessary. Impala (and Caprice) also implemented a new four-speed automatic transmission with overdrive and torque-converter clutch.

Manufacturers continued to downsize their cars as the early 1980s rolled toward mid-decade. Rumors were once again swirling around that the Impala/Caprice platform was to be discontinued. Annual face-lifts since the 1977 redesign had done little to change the car. By 1982 Chevy was introducing a new subcompact called the Cavalier and a new midsize named the Celebrity. New nameplates, new technology—where did the Impala, with its roots in the 1950s, fit in? The only models wearing the Impala nameplate in 1982 were a four-door sedan and a station wagon. Sedan sales, traditionally strong for Impala, couldn't climb above 50,000, but then none of Chevy's other best-selling models could punch out the 100,000-car barrier.

In 1983 a four-door sedan was all that was left for Impala. It was the same way that Biscayne and Bel Air had bowed out in the 1970s. The popularity of sport sedans, or sport anything for that matter, was not advancing during these tough economic times. Where did the Impala fit in? The answer was: It didn't. Without so much as a farewell tour, Chevy turned ut the lights on Impala. A legitimate question was: Would anyone care?

Some of That Old Magic Returns

"The roots of true achievement lie in the will to become the best that you can become."

—Harold Taylor

It was as if Elvis had entered the building. The King was back. And, damn, he looked good! A lot of people probably thought they'd never see the day when another Impala SS would leap onto the stage. After all, almost a quarter century had played out since Chevy last brought a crowd to its feet with a performance-minded Impala, an enthusiast's car with the moxie to blow the doors off any other car in its class.

The 1994 Chevrolet Impala SS was a shot of adrenaline for American auto buyers who were nostalgic about the days when real musclecars roamed the roads and the original Impala SS of 409 fame ruled the planet. Years and years of bland cars, stripped of emotion, had been

When the Impala returned to the scene in 1994, there was a concerted effort to relive the glory days when the car was big and fast and at one glance everyone knew this car's name. Driving enthusiasts with some money in their pocket were choosing sport sedans as their weapon of choice, so Chevy did what needed to be done—they gave the four-door Caprice body a decent set of clothes, dropped in a 5.7-liter Corvette engine, tweaked the suspension, and set it on some fat rubber. Instant cult classic. *Zone Five Photo*

Inside the Impala SS the comfort level was dialed up a notch from the average Chevrolet. The standard equipment list included four-speed automatic transmission, AM/FM stereo tape player, air conditioning, cruise control, dual air bag restraints, leather seats, power driver seat, power door locks, power mirrors, power windows, remote trunk release, theft deterrent system, tilt steering wheel, and tinted glass. *Zone Five Photo*

endured. Some would say the 1970s and 1980s produced far more practical automobiles than the previous two decades. OK. Fine. But another way to describe them would be cars shackled by government fuel economy regulations and a social climate that fostered standardization. And, you notice, I didn't use any cuss words.

The new Impala proved that after a steady diet of hamburger, there were some hungry people who were craving steak. Technology, sophistication, and safety were the side dishes that complemented the meat.

Chevrolet had invented the full-size American performance car of the 1990s. Not from a clean sheet of paper, but more in the likeness of the 1958 Impala that was actually a special edition. In that case, Impala sprang from the popular Bel Air line. It was truly a car set apart from the rest, with significant features, not just decals and paint. When the 1994 Impala SS was rolled out, some would say

Previous Page
For three years, 1994 through 1996, the Impala SS was back on the street. It was a headline car. Chevrolet got face time in all the motoring press and major newspapers around the world. Chevy enthusiasts who had survived the 1980s automotive wasteland got ready to rock 'n' roll again. *Zone Five Photo*

it was nothing less than magic that had transformed an uninteresting Caprice Classic into a nasty-looking, sweet-handling modern musclecar. In 1958 the sport coupe was the rage. In 1994 the sport sedan was the choice ride.

Back in the late 1950s and throughout the 1960s, Chevrolet built the SS models with panache. Today it's called attitude. They were factory hot rods, but they included many features—both inside and out—that contributed mightily to the car's image. Those that are reverently remembered were loaded with power and heavy-duty suspension parts, but even the dressed-for-show-and-not-to-go SS models maintained a high degree of distinction and respect. People took notice of an SS on the street. It captured attention when it passed by and, better yet, when you sat inside. The new Impala ably carried that torch.

For starters, the latest Impala SS was nobody's nerdy cousin from Hicksville. Chevy made sure of that by dropping a nearly identical twin to the Corvette LT1 engine into the mix. The LT1 comes from one of the all-time great Chevy engines, the small-block 350-ci (5.7 liter) V-8. It will never have the cut-throat, killer drag-racing reputation of the 409, but its acceleration is damn near as good and it makes a better-balanced road car than the big block. If you're interested in such things, the LT1 kicks butt in a fuel economy com-

Seventeen-inch wheels and a modified police-package suspension added serious grip to the standard Caprice setup. The Impala SS was a musclecar for the 1990s, a performance car that wasn't confined to racing in a straight line. *Zone Five Photo*

parison. The 260 horsepower isn't on call for any economy runs, but its sequential fuel injection is far more efficient at shooting the juice than a pair of Rochester four barrels. It also runs on regular unleaded, as opposed to the aviation fuel required for the classic high-compression musclecar engines. A 10.5:1 compression was used in the 1994 SS, which also featured a cast-iron block and cast-aluminum heads.

To go along with the giddy-up, it was wisely determined to use a modified police car suspension (the Caprice was a notable and noticeable patrol car of its era), and larger-than-standard 17-inch wheels with sticky tires. The Impala SS handled very well, even on a twisty road; the ride was firm and sports car–like. The P255/50 ZR17 tires courtesy of B. F. Goodrich were a real benefit.

Viewed in terms of its performance, it was a police special without a light bar stuck to the roof. In *Motor Trend* magazine testing, reported in the June 1994 issue, they whipped the SS to a 7.1-second 0–60 time. Airing it out in the quarter mile, the SS tripped the lights at 91.1 miles per hour, covering the distance in 15.4 seconds. "Significantly quicker," *Motor Trend* reported, "than the legendary SS396 Impalas of yore."

Whereas the original musclecars were lionized for breakneck acceleration, they were seldom praised for stellar braking capabilities or composed handling. That's an area

where 25 years of suspension technological focus had produced some monumental changes for the better. Begin with four-wheel, anti-lock disc brakes with 12.1-inch rotors. If there's nostalgia for drum brakes on all four wheels, it's a select group of grizzled old horses who probably prefer solid

1994 Impala SS Standard Equipment

Engine: 8-cylinder 5.7-liters (350 ci)
Transmission: four-speed automatic
Accessories: AM/FM stereo with cassette tape, air conditioning, aluminum alloy wheels, anti-lock brakes, cruise control, digital clock, dual air bag restraints, intermittent wipers, leather seats, limited-slip differential, power brakes, power door locks, power driver seat, power mirrors, power steering, power windows, rear spoiler, remote trunk release, theft-deterrent system, tilt steering wheel, and tinted glass

The transformation of the rather dull Caprice was accomplished by adding five-spoke aluminum alloy wheels, low-profile tires, showing them off by opening up the wheelwells, modifying the rear quarter windows, and selecting a dark-colored paint. The 1994 Impala SS was available only in monochrome black. In 1995 dark cherry and dark green-gray were added to the mix. *Zone Five Photo*

rubber tires as well. Cornering with the old coil spring and solid rear axle cars resulted in body roll that is beyond comprehension when compared to the modern Impala, even though the coil springs and solid rear axle remained all these years. A limited-slip differential (Posi-Traction still sounds good) helped get power to the ground, where tire technology was responsible for giant strides in driving improvements. The transmission was a four-speed automatic.

There are many valid comparisons to the original Impala of 1958. To begin with, both were conceived as concept cars for the major auto shows. Both cars accomplished a great deal with relatively few cosmetic changes from their predecessors. In 1958 the Impala advantages included unique spinner-type wheel covers, a modified upper body structure that gave the car a lower profile, a six-taillight configuration, a more sumptuous interior with colorful fabrics and a sporty steering wheel, and additional trim items that were highly desirable at that time. The modern Impala took advantage of classy five-spoke, 17-inch aluminum alloy wheels and low-profile tires fully exposed by cutaway wheel arches. Minor body modifications— modi-

1995 Impala SS Specifications

Base price: $22,910
Engine type: Overhead valve, fuel-injected V-8
Engine size: 5.7 liters/350 ci
Horsepower: 260 @ 4,800 rpm
Torque: 330 ft/lb @ 3,200 rpm
Drive train: Front engine/rear drive
Transmission: Four-speed automatic
  w/overdrive
Wheelbase/Length: 116 inches/214 inches
Tires: BF Goodrich Z24 Comp
  T/A P255/50 ZR17
Brakes: Anti-lock vented discs standard
Curb weight: 4,200 pounds
Fuel capacity: 23 gallons
Fuel requirement: Unleaded regular
  (87 octane)
Miles per gallon: 17 city, 25 highway

fied rear quarter windows, a small ducktail spoiler on the rear deck—contributed greatly. The ominous-looking black paint job with just the right touch when it came to badges was well executed to convey the car's powerful image.

Inside the Impala SS, leather-trimmed upholstery was a standout feature that represented a high level of quality. The leather-wrapped steering wheel was a noteworthy addition, too, as was the full-length console.

The interior felt roomy because this was a big automobile. It shared its basic platform with the Buick Roadmaster and the Cadillac Fleetwood—cars that were built with comfort in mind. Impala gets extra credit in this area for its contoured seats (front and back), which were appreciably more comfortable than the standard issue stuff.

There was also a full complement of classy accessories as standard equipment: power windows, locks, and mirrors, power front seats, plus infra-red remote locking. An attractive center console (with cup holders, but not in the underside of

the glovebox lid), a leather-wrapped steering wheel, and a blacked-out instrument panel provided the touches that result in pride of ownership. Sound systems were another major improvement from the days of the wondrous 8-track player. No performance comparison here: The AM/FM/CD stereo poured out high-quality sound. Controlling the climate with the heater and air conditioner was easy and far more comfortable than what was offered in the good old days.

Safety concerns were formerly addressed with lap belts and padded instrument panels. In 1994 the Impala offered dual front airbags, three-point outboard seat belts with a height adjustment for the front seats, and rear-door child-safety locks. The design of the body structure incorporated steel safety-cage construction plus front and rear crush zones and side-impact protection.

Optional equipment included a combination AM/FM radio and compact disc player, a keyless entry system, a power antenna, a power passenger seat, and a rear window defroster.

The Impala SS returned for 1995 with few changes. Two new colors—a dark cherry and green-gray—were added to the original basic black. A slight redesign of the seats improved comfort, and improvements to the audio system included a speed-compensated volume control. For more convenience in tight storage situations, the outside rearview mirrors could be folded.

In 1996 a 4.3-liter, 16-valve V-8 engine rated at 200 horsepower became optional. Although the complaints have not been loud or long, Chevy listened to the pleas of the enthusiasts who asked that a tachometer be added to the instrument cluster, and a floor shifter grace the center console. It seemed this car was just getting a fine tuning when the decision was made to discontinue it. Great looks, great performance, and a nice price that could make owners laugh about what some of the other sport sedan buyers were shelling out weren't enough to save the Impala SS from the gallows.

CHAPTER 9

The Next Generation

"Nostalgia is okay but not what it used to be."

—*Anonymous*

As a testimony to the lasting impression of the Impala name and a nod toward re-establishing Chevrolet as an image car, General Motors reintroduced the Impala in mid-1999 as a 2000 model. Five and one-half years had slipped by since the last Impala received its badges. That car was the much-revered, performance-oriented Impala SS sport sedan. The latest Impala, like its successor, was introduced in a single body style—four-door sedan.

Among enthusiasts the Impala SS is practically worshipped, and an Impala without hearty performance attributes is an Impala without heart. That highly publicized and widely held perception is a main ingredient in the Impala magic. In the big scheme of things, however, Impala has been a lot of things to a lot of people. Still, its credentials as a handsome, dependable family car that represents a good value for the money were responsible for most sales.

That's what the 2000 Impala is all about. Its attention to comfort, convenience, safety, and quality makes an enticing package, and it easily exceeds the early Impalas in each of those areas. On the modern playing

Chevrolet delivered the 2000 Impala to dealerships in June 1999, but it was being displayed on the car show circuit six months before that. It is shown here at the Los Angeles Auto Show in January 2000. *Zone Five Photo*

119

Just like the original Impala, the 2000 version offers a lot of car for the money. It is a blend of style, performance, quality, safety, and comfort. *Zone Five Photo*

field for midsize cars, four-door sedans dominate the action, and the new Impala was designed and built to rule this territory.

The Impala tradition is branded with accomplishments. And with each achievement, the success of the four-door sedan was prominent. Yet its automotive legacy was not built on four-door sedans. It was always more. When borrowing from tradition, the best parts can't be ignored. For those who grew up with Impala, the badge signifies a standout in the categories of good looks and athletic prowess. When originally introduced in 1958, the Impala was clearly something special—a sporty car that was daringly different and not afraid to stand out from the crowd. All the original Impalas were either sport coupes or convertibles. In the late 1950s, that was the style that signified success. It was also a time when power and performance in a Chevrolet could match just about

anything else on the road, regardless of price. The original Impala rumbled with plenty of horsepower, including the optional 348-ci V-8 with tri-power carbs. Even in its most recent incarnation—the early 1990s Impala SS sedan—there was clearly an emphasis on sport, with plenty of special features, including that throbbing LT-1 Corvette engine.

With this newest of Impalas, Chevrolet has a fine performance-oriented car, but one without a knock-out punch. It has a lot to offer, but at the same time, maybe not quite enough. The Impala image and heritage have not been completely fulfilled. It's on the board, but it's not a bull's eye. This is first and foremost a traditional family sedan. It makes no bold statements and easily blends into a parking lot full of modern domestic and import sedans. Chevrolet built an excellent car, but not a particularly exciting one. It's capable. It's quicker than most in its class. It's fun to drive. In many ways it's so much better than the Impalas of old. But in many ways it is so much less compelling.

The latest in the Impala lineage is a completely different breed. The new version follows the industry-wide trend of powering the front wheels. That makes it the first Impala to not be driven by its rear wheels. And in keeping with cars in its class, no more than six cylinders are put into action. In this case it's a V-6, which comes in two flavors—mild and medium hot. Looking back at Impala's best years, there was an excitement and a pride of ownership derived from performance standards and styling leadership. Those qualities come up big when borrowing from tradition. This Impala does everything it's supposed to, and it does it better than most of the competition. You gotta like it for what it is, what it does, and how well it does it. It's still the heartbeat of America, even if it just doesn't cause your heart to beat as fast as the Impalas of old.

There is a bit of Impala retrospective with the round headlights and taillights that are less than obvious lurking within modern plastic facades. Step on the brakes and the surprisingly large, circular taillights jump out, making the Impala easy to spot in traffic. John Cafaro, Chevrolet Studio Design Chief, said his team took inspiration from the 1965 Impala, the most popular Impala of all time.

"The '65 Impala was so clean and uncluttered," Cafaro said. "I can still remember that Impala from when

2000 Specifications

Body Style:
Base model — six-passenger sedan
LS model — five-passenger sedan
Engine:
Base model — 3.4-liter ohv V-6
    180 hp/205 ft-lb
LS model — 3.8-liter ohv V-6 200 hp/225 ft-lb
Drive/Trans: four-speed automatic
Suspension, front/rear: Strut/Strut
Wheelbase: 110.5 inches
Curb weight: 3,389 pounds
Length: 200 inches
Width: 73 inches
Height: 57.5 inches
Track, front/rear: 62.0/61.3 inches
Brakes, front/rear: Disc/Disc, ABS
Tires: 225/60R16
Cargo capacity: 17.6 cu. ft.
Restraints: Dual air bags,
    Front-seat side air bags
Fuel economy, city/hwy: 19/29 mpg (est.)

Large, round taillights are distinctive and help Impala stand out from the pack when the driver steps on the brakes. Two taillights per side, however, don't mesh with the Impala tradition. *Zone Five Photo*

The interior is roomy, comfortable, and convenient. For a modern midsize car, it is surprisingly spacious. Seats were not much concern in the classic Impalas, but were well planned for the 2000. *Zone Five Photo*

I was a kid, and it made a big impression on me." He said the design effort wanted to "communicate that same clean contemporary attitude in this new car."

In the designing of this all-new Impala, Cafaro relied on sharply sculpted exterior lines, particularly in the rear quarters. "It was our job, visually, to tell the story of performance and stability. We've done that with a low and very wide stance, and by making the outside plane of the tires the outermost plane of the vehicle. Then we shaved the skin around that." Accentuating the stance is a low-slung front fascia and a wedge shape that culminates in a high deck lid. Compared to competitors like the Ford

Previous Page
The base engine is a 180-horsepower six cylinder, with a 200-horsepower six available in the LS version. The bow-tie logo and bar across the grille is one effort to connect to Impala's heritage. *Zone Five Photo*

Taurus and Toyota Avalon, the Impala appearance can accurately be described as aggressive. There is an undeniable swagger that plays well. Much of the car's character is provided by the large, 16-inch wheels and P225/60R16 tires (standard on the LS) and clean, aerodynamic exterior. Compared to the 1960s production standards that allowed many variances in fit and finish, the 2000 Impala shows a world of improvement.

Two models are available: the base Impala ($19,265) and the LS ($22,925). The LS features the 200-horsepower, 3.8-liter V-6 engine as standard equipment. It also brings to the table aluminum wheels, a quicker steering ratio, traction control, anti-lock brakes, and a wide range of electric amenities. The base 3.4-liter V-6, standard in the base Impala, produces 180 horsepower. The big V-6 is an option in the base Impala. Both engines feature sequential fuel injection. Also standard are platinum-tipped spark plugs and extended-life coolant and transmission fluid, which the factory says are good for 100,000 miles without replacement.

Standard features that are indicative of the time lapse since the debut of the previous Impala include a 17-item message center; a radio/data-system stereo; three rear-seat child-seat tethers; a passlock theft deterrent; and daytime running lights. Additional niceties include air conditioning; a rear defogger; power locks, mirrors, and windows; a 60/40 front bench seat; and body side moldings. The message center display provides warnings about such things as the need for an oil change or a possible loss of coolant.

Optional equipment includes an overhead console; dual-zone climate control; an air filtration system (standard on the LS); CD stereo; leather upholstery; leather-wrapped steering wheel; and an engine-block heater. The interior materials reflect quality and thoughtfulness. The padded dash top is well made, large analog gauges are easy to see, and controls are placed in logical, convenient locations.

Trim levels are base and LS, separated mostly by powertrain. The base model has a 180-horsepower 3.4-liter V-6, the LS a 200-horsepower 3.8-liter V-6. Torque ratings are 205 foot-pounds and 225 foot-pounds, respectively. The bigger engine is optional on the base model. With the bigger V-6, the Impala is quicker than the six-seat models from Toyota, Dodge, Ford, and Buick. The 2000 Impala V-6 engines are larger displacement versions (larger cylinder bores) of the 3100 series V-6. They also have higher compression ratios than the 3100. The free-revving engines (6,000 rpm redline) continue to have pushrod-activated valves rather than the more common overhead camshaft designs. The camshaft is chain driven and uses hydraulic, roller-type lifters. Engine construction consists of cast-iron blocks with aluminum heads.

A Hydra-Matic transmission is standard on all Impalas. It's an electronically controlled, four-speed automatic transaxle type with a final drive ratio of 2.86:1 (3400 V-6) and 3.05:1 (3800 V-6).

The Impala has a big-car appearance even though it's nowhere close in overall dimensions to big Impalas of the late 1950s and 1960s. Much of the stature comes from its upright windows, its roof pillars and longer greenhouse. Sight lines forward and to the side are good, and excellent mirror location provides confidence when wondering what's out of range of your peripheral vision. The high rear deck lid requires some getting used to with regard to the view through the rear window.

Interior space and driver/passenger comfort are the car's finest points. The Impala has a noticeably high roofline, the opposite effect of early Impalas when the styling objective was to lower the roofline each year. Inside the car, it feels even larger than expected.

Base models come with a split bench in the front that accommodates three-across seating. Although the seats look flat, they feel like bucket seats and provide good support. The five-passenger LS models offer two bucket seats up front with a spacious center console, although the bench seat is optional. The rear seat is split 60/40, and folds down to allow lengthy items to protrude from the trunk. Rear-seat comfort has also been enhanced by slightly raising the seat, which provides a better line of sight for passengers.

Designing a comfortable seat was a high priority for the 2000 Impala. Forty years earlier the only difference between the seats in an Impala and the lower-priced models was an extra layer of padding. The new Impala seats are the result of one of the most extensive research and testing programs ever conducted for a GM sedan. They are better shaped to supply thigh and lateral support, and even the seams and sewing patterns were taken into account.

Laudable engineering features that bolster the Impala's stock include a substantial, extruded aluminum engine-cradle that secures the drivetrain. It's substantially lighter and stiffer than a steel component, and is more corrosion resistant. That structure combined with the magnesium dashboard bulkhead (Chevy refers to it as the MagBeam instrument panel support) creates a rigid but lightweight structure that provides a solid and secure road feel. Another engineering feature is the strut tower crossbrace that reduces body twisting. It's a handling enhancement found in most high-performance cars, but seldom included in family sedans.

On the road, the Impala is both quick and agile, in a way that could not have been dreamed of in the days of the first Impalas. There's really no comparison to the Impalas of old, just as those cars were light years ahead of the cars that predated them by 40 years. Decades of engineering improvements put things in a new perspective. The LS benefits from its quicker steering ratio, but both models employ a strut brace in front and anti-roll bars front and rear. All Impalas benefit from a firm independent suspension, a trailing-arm design that is much beefier than previous units. Impala suspension utilizes struts at all four corners, four-wheel disc brakes, 16-inch wheels and tires, and rack-and-pinion power-assisted steering. The LS models are equipped with a touring suspension that uses higher-rate springs for more body-roll control. The base Impala gets steel wheels with bolt-on plastic wheel covers, while the LS wears five-spoke aluminum alloy wheels.

From a dead stop, full acceleration will get your attention (zero to 60 miles per hour comes under 8 seconds), but without a true high-performance engine, it lacks the enthusiasm that was generated by the legendary V-8 engines that prowled the streets back in the 1960s. The modern V-6 is geared to get off the line quickly, but it wasn't designed to match the straight-line performance

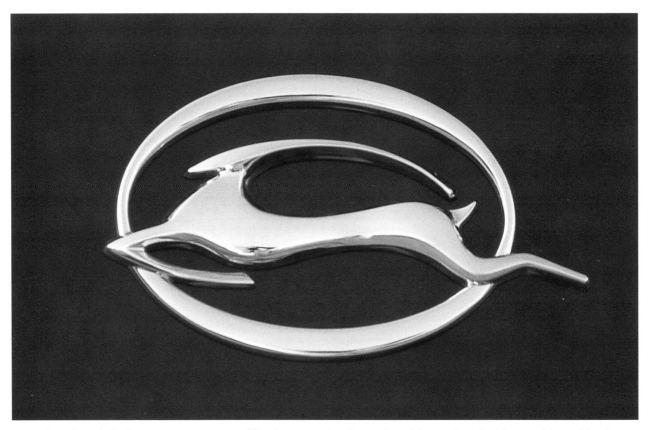

The traditional Impala badge conjures up memories of the glory years when the Impala and the Impala SS had the rest of the world in their hip pockets. *Zone Five Photo*

of big-muscle mills of yore. On the other hand, the fuel-injected six will loaf along at 70 miles per hour all day long, and can triple or quadruple the gas mileage of the old monsters. Reliability is far better, and the reduction in emissions is laudable. The 2000 Impala also gives the driver something no other Impala ever has—torque steer. This is the first front-wheel-drive Impala ever. Long-time Impala enthusiasts decry the loss of rear-wheel drive, but with 85 percent of all cars using front-wheel drive, Impala is in line with popular thinking.

"When it comes to performance, today's sedan buyers want more than just horsepower," said Don Parkinson, the Impala brand manager. "They want refined road manners, agile handling, and superb braking performance."

"Impala is tied together structurally the way a great driver's car should be," said chief engineer Greg Bellopatrick. "We've been able to leverage Impala's structural improvements into a quiet ride, agile handling, and enhanced vehicle quality."

Disc brakes on all four wheels is a real enhancement. It uses brake rotors that are huge for a car its size, and the pads and calipers are designed to withstand abusive conditions.

The anti-lock brake system is standard in cars equipped with the big six-cylinder engine. And that system also includes a tire-pressure warning monitor.

Safety features include safety-cage construction, energy-absorbing side-impact protection, daytime running lamps, a padded headliner and ceiling, and an optional seat-mounted side air bag for the driver.

The National Highway Traffic Safety Administration gave the 2000 Impala a five-star rating for protecting both the driver and the front-seat passenger in a head-on collision.

When the Impala was first conceived as a 1958 model, chief engineer Ed Cole said the mission was to build "a prestige car within the reach of the average American citizen." By the year 2000, with the Impala name badges dusted off and reissued on a mainstream American sedan, Chevy still has a great car at a great price. Will the new Impala attain the American icon status of the original Impala? That remains to be seen. Times have changed, and so has the Impala. The formula for success still applies. And the Impala name still has a special place in the hearts of many Americans. I would not bet against the magic it possesses.

The Tradition Lives On

The Late Great Chevy Club is a worldwide organization of Chevy enthusiasts who are particularly interested in the years 1958 through 1964. The group has been affiliated since 1980. Although the members show an appreciation for all Chevrolet vehicles, the ones that stand out are the Impalas.

Robert Snowden and Danny Howell are both officers and founders of the organization. In their 19 years of involvement with the cars and the people who love these cars, they have gained some good insight into how these automobiles are viewed today.

In terms of collectibility, Snowden said, "since day one, the most popular cars have been the '64s." These cars have always enjoyed a high level of attention. It's not too surprising to learn that the convertibles, especially those with the 409 engine, are the biggest hits. The Impala Super Sport models, across all years, are "the most sought after and the most desired." After all of those are claimed, he suspects, the 1964 sport coupes and the remaining Impalas in good condition will become hot commodities.

One of the best things about a 1964, Howell said, is that "you can jump in and drive it across the country." The cars are comfortably equipped with items such as good-quality factory air conditioning, power steering, power brakes, and AM/FM radio. "You have all the creature comforts you want," Howell said. "These options became standard fare in Chevrolets in the early 1960s. I think it's what made it America's car."

The most expensive cars, however, are the 1958 Impala convertibles. They are a very difficult car to find, and because they are rare the value is high—as high or higher than any other collectible Chevrolet (not counting the most rare Corvettes). "Some guys have done incredible restoration projects to save a '58 Impala convertible," Snowden said.

"Chevy hit on something with the introduction of the Impala in 1958," Howell said. "The Impala has had a continuous increase in interest and popularity among the hobbyists. In the market today, a '58 Impala convertible will command as much as a 1957 Bel Air. But finding a '57 convertible is much easier than finding a '58 convertible. The fact is that more '58s were built than '57s. Probably three or four times more '57s have been collected than '58s. Really junked out cars are being bought today, because they are so hard to find."

Howell said much of the appeal for the 1958 Impala comes from the fact that it has the first of the Chevy big-block engines. The displacement was 348 ci, and the most collectible version has tri-power (three two-barrel carburetors). Another factor in the popularity of the 1958 is that it's so gaudy. All that chrome and trim, Howell says, "captures a certain imagination." It was more like a Cadillac than any other Chevy of that era.

When the Late Great organization was founded in 1980, the 1964 Chevy was only 16 years old. Cars that new are generally not considered classics, but today that car is more than 35 years old. As time marches on, newer cars become collectible. That's why Snowden and Howell formed another group called Yesteryear Chevys. This Chevy-lovers organization takes the next step by honoring the 1965 through 1972 Chevrolets.

"These cars aren't typically getting the frame-off restorations yet," Snowden said. "But they will definitely be the next ones."

Chevrolet put many good cars on the street in the 1960s, and there are a lot of people who would love to have one today. It's a tribute to an ongoing success story.

"Chevy managed to nurture the Impala—a high-end car—for the blue-collar worker in America," Howell noted. He couldn't have been more right about that.

For more information on Impalas from 1958 through 1972, contact: Late Great Chevys, P.O. Box 607824, Orlando, FL 32806; telephone: 407/886-1963.

INDEX